# READING SKILLS FOR SUCCESS

## A Guide to Academic Texts

THOMAS A. UPTON

THE UNIVERSITY OF MICHIGAN PRESS
Ann Arbor

To Mary
my wife and best friend

# Preface

*Reading Skills for Success* is unique in that it provides a guide for teaching reading skills to college and precollege students that can be used with most any freshman-level academic material, whether it be a textbook that students are using for another class (e.g., Introduction to Psychology), an eclectic mix of texts from a variety of outside classes, or other teacher-collected material. This textbook is designed so that teachers can work through specific reading strategies with students, use the general activities and sample academic chapters to practice the strategies being taught, and then have the students turn to their outside readings (e.g., academic texts, journals) to put into practice the strategies they are learning.

The goal of *Reading Skills for Success* is to help students make the transition from the "sheltered" reading material provided in many precollege and ESL classes to the material that they are expected to work with in mainstream academic settings. This text should be viewed, and used, as an adjunct text to assist students in comprehending the material they are expected to read in college "content" classes. *Reading Skills for Success* is designed so that students at the undergraduate, community college, and advanced high school levels can apply the strategies and skills introduced in this book to the reading materials they need to master in other courses.

*Reading Skills for Success* is aimed at students in the following contexts:

1. ESL and other precollege reading level students in reading classes connected to academic classes (e.g., Sociology, Psychology).
2. ESL and other precollege reading level students taking reading classes but also taking or preparing to take college-level academic classes for the first time.
3. Students in English for Special Purposes (ESP) courses that have no appropriate ESL textbook on the topic being studied.
4. Students in advanced high school and community college reading courses designed to prepare students for college-level reading.

Classes like these can be found in most ESL programs, community colleges, high schools, and college academic skills centers.

## Approach and Overview

The chapters in *Reading Skills for Success* use as their foundation the current understanding that reading is an interactive and constructive process in which the reader uses personal and cultural knowledge to interpret the information presented in a text in order to "create" meaning. For many weaker readers and nonnative speakers of English, much of their miscomprehension when reading English academic texts is due to their inability to recognize word and structural clues that native speakers readily process. Particularly in academic settings, reading miscomprehension often occurs not so much because of a lack of cultural or content knowledge—in academic classes most information is new to all students—but because of a lack of text-based, linguistic preparedness necessary to quickly spot key information and organizational structure in texts.

*Reading Skills for Success* helps students focus on and develop these text-based processing skills while teachers provide the necessary assistance with background and interpretation for the specific materials students need to read. To this end, this book addresses in part 1 **word-level clues** that students need to learn to look for as they read. Part 2 is designed to introduce students to the **different types of expository text structures** they will need to recognize as they begin intensive analytical reading of academic prose. Last, part 3 focuses on helping students go about the job of **studying.** The goal when reading academic texts goes beyond simple comprehension; students are frequently required to take the information they are reading and apply it in some way, either in papers or in response to exam questions. Part 3 focuses on reading strategies that assist in the in-depth and long-term understanding of long and complex academic texts.

A major strength of this book is the extensive use of excerpts from actual textbooks used in first-year college courses, including complete chapters from a textbook on environmental sciences and from a textbook on human geography, which are found in the appendixes. Because the material in the appendixes is excerpted from full-length textbooks, these chapters contain cross-references to materials (figures, tables, textbook pages, etc.) that are not included in this book. These cross-references have been retained because students need to become familiar with the use of cross-references in academic material and because this maintains the integrity of the chapters as they were originally written.

I would like to thank Pam Ruble for her extensive help, discussion, and suggestions while I was writing this book. Thanks also to Melanie Curfman, who helped me type and check lists, and who protected me from outside distractions so that I could work. Many thanks also to my students through the years who tested much of the material and suggested improvements to the activities.

Thanks to my family—my wife, Mary, and my children, Nicholas and Peter—who have helped me learn that there is more to life than deadlines, and a special thanks to my parents, Richard and Marjorie, who have always encouraged and supported me.

*Grateful acknowledgment is made to the following authors, publishers, and journals for permission to reprint previously published materials.*

American Association for the Advancement of Science for "language families" figure. Reprinted with permission from R. Lewin, "American Indian Language Dispute," *Science* 242 (1988): 1633. Copyright © 1988, American Association for the Advancement of Science.

Thomas Moore for images from "The Early History of Indo-European Languages," by T. V. Gamkrelidze and V. V. Ivanov from *Scientific American,* March 1990, copyright © 1990.

Pearson Education for *Environmental Science: The Way the World Works,* 6/E by Nebel/Wright, copyright © 1998. Reprinted by permission of Pearson Education, Inc., Upper Saddle River, NJ.

Scientific American for illustrations by Johnny Johnson from "The Origins of Indo-Languages," by Colin Renfrew, October 1989, copyright © 1989, and from "The Austronesian Dispersal and the Origin of Languages," by Peter Bellwood, July 1991, copyright © 1991.

John Wiley & Sons for material from *Human Geography: Culture, Society, and Space;* "The Diffusion of Languages," by H. J. de Blij and Alexander B. Murphy. Copyright © 1999 John Wiley & Sons. This material is used by permission of John Wiley & Sons, Inc.

Ian Warpole for image from "Hard Words," by Phillip E. Ross, from *Scientific American,* April 1991, copyright © 1991.

*Every effort has been made to trace the ownership of all copyrighted material in this book and to obtain permission for its use.*

# Contents

# Part 1
# WORD-LEVEL CLUES TO MEANING

To be a good reader, you must have the following:

- the ability to quickly recognize words and their meanings,
- knowledge about how texts are structured, and
- knowledge about the content that is being presented.

The three chapters in part 1 will help you develop the first element—the ability to more quickly recognize words and their meanings.

**Chapter 1** focuses on helping you expand your vocabulary. It has two goals:

- to help you learn important vocabulary words that are typically used in textbooks; and
- to show you how to better use context to guess the meaning of words you don't know.

**Chapter 2** looks at technical vocabulary. Many readers miss the definitions of technical terms that are typically given in textbooks because they do not recognize that a definition is being given. This chapter shows you the many different ways that academic writers define key terms.

**Chapter 3** focuses on the use of pronouns and restatements. One major source of miscomprehension for inexperienced readers is their inability to recognize the continuation of key ideas in a text through the use of pronouns and other ways of restating ideas. This chapter introduces and gives you practice with recognizing and understanding the many ways that academic texts restate ideas.

# Chapter 1 Vocabulary Development Strategies: Using Context Clues

A limited vocabulary may be the single most difficult problem developing readers face. The well-prepared native speaker of English entering college knows about twenty thousand words. Unfortunately, many developing readers, including ESL students, have a much more limited vocabulary. The good news is that only two thousand words make up 76 percent of those we encounter as we read.[1] These high-frequency words are ones like *the, these, many,* and *is.* Most likely, you already know most, if not all, of these two thousand high-frequency words.

Another bit of good news is that by learning an additional 570 word families[2] common in academic texts, you will know over 86 percent of the words you will read in academic textbooks (Coxhead 2000). The other 14 percent of words in academic texts are technical words that are usually new for every student and defined in the texts or low-frequency words that you won't see very often. Nevertheless, you will need to learn these technical and low-frequency words in order to excel in school.

This chapter will look first at some of the academic words you should learn and then will discuss strategies that you can use to help you learn these words and the other low-frequency words that you will encounter. Strategies for recognizing and learning technical terms that are specific to a particular field of study will be explored in chapter 2.

---

1. Averil Coxhead, "A New Academic Word List," *TESOL Quarterly* 34, no. 2 (2000): 213–38.
2. A word family is a group of words with a common base and related meanings; for example, the following words make up a single word family: *indicate, indicated, indicating, indication, indications, indicative, indicator, indicators.* Once you learn the meaning of one of these words, you will be able to easily figure out what the other words in the family mean.

## Explanation and Examples

There is no magic way to easily learn new words. Learning vocabulary is hard work and takes time. But what does it mean to "know" a word? Obviously, it means recognizing a word when we see or hear it. But to know a word, we need to not only recognize it, but understand what it means and how to use it. To know a word well, we should also know what other words are used with it (*student* often occurs with *teacher*) and what other forms it may have (*love, lovely, lovable, loving, lovingly*).

To build your vocabulary, you must develop a system to help you review and remember the new words you encounter. There are many ways to keep a record of new words, and you should choose one that works well for you. One common method is to use flash cards. On the front of the card you write the word and below it the pronunciation, if you need help remembering it. On the back, indicate the part of speech (for example, adjective), the meaning, an example of the word in a sentence, and some of its other common forms. A vocabulary card might look like the following.

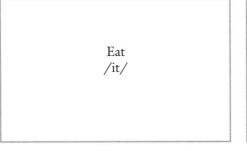

|  |  |
|---|---|
| Eat /it/ | Verb: past- ate; participle- eaten<br>Meaning: to take food into the mouth; chew; consume<br>"I like to eat fish for dinner."<br>Other forms:<br>  (adj) edible /ɛdəbəl/ |
| **Front** | **Back** |

**Activity →** Table 1.1 lists 300 of the most common academic words that students need to know and know how to use, along with the related forms of the word family. (Table D.1 in supplement D provides a list of 270 more words.) Obviously, you are not going to be able to learn all these words at one time, but you can start learning them a few at a time. In a few weeks, you should be familiar with most of them.

1. Look through the academic words in table 1.1. Make flash cards for 25 words that you already know and feel comfortable using and then review them. If you don't already know 25 of the words, pick any 25, make flash cards for them, and start studying them. This stack of flash cards will be your **new word pile.** Study your new word pile as often as you can, at least once a day.

2. At least once a week, write the words in your new word pile on a sheet of paper. *Without looking at your cards,* see if you can write the definition and an original sentence or two using the word so that it clearly shows that you understand what the word means and how to use it. Underline the word in the sentence. If you know more than one meaning for the word or have learned its different forms, give an example for all meanings and forms.

**TABLE 1.1   300 Common Academic Words** (Adapted from Coxhead 2000)

NOTE: The different forms of these words should be learned as well as the form listed here. For example, when learning *access*, you should also learn *accesses*, *accessing*, and *accessible*.

**A**
academy
access
achieve
acquire
adequate
adjust
administrate
affect
alter
alternative
amend
analyze
annual
apparent
approach
appropriate
approximate
area
aspect
assess
assist
assume
attitude
attribute
authority
available
aware

**B**
benefit

**C**
capacity
category
challenge
chapter
circumstance
civil
clause
code
comment
commission
commit
communicate
community
compensate
complex

component
compound
compute
concentrate
concept
conclude
conduct
confer
conflict
consent
consequent
considerable
consist
constant
constitute
constrain
construct
consult
consume
contact
context
contract
contrast
contribute
convene
coordinate
core
corporate
correspond
create
credit
criteria
culture
cycle

**D**
data
debate
decline
deduce
define
demonstrate
derive
design
despite
dimension
discreet
distinct

distribute
document
domestic
dominate
draft

**E**
economy
element
emerge
emphasis
enable
energy
enforce
ensure
entity
environment
equate
equivalent
error
establish
estimate
ethnic
evaluate
evident
evolve
exclude
expand
export
expose
external

**F**
facilitate
factor
feature
final
finance
focus
formula
framework
function
fund
fundamental

**G**
generate
generation

goal
grant

**H**
hence
hypothesis

**I**
identify
illustrate
image
immigrate
impact
implement
implicate
imply
impose
income
indicate
individual
initial
injure
instance
institute
integrate
interact
internal
interpret
invest
investigate
involve
issue
item

**J**
job
journal
justify

**L**
label
labor
layer
legal
legislate
liberal
license
link

*(continued)*

**TABLE 1.1—*Continued***

| | | | |
|---|---|---|---|
| locate | partner | reject | style |
| logic | perceive | relevant | subsequent |
| | percent | rely | substitute |
| **M** | period | remove | sufficient |
| maintain | perspective | require | sum |
| major | phase | research | summary |
| margin | philosophy | reside | survey |
| maximize | physical | resolve | sustain |
| mechanism | policy | resource | symbol |
| medical | positive | respond | |
| mental | potential | restrict | **T** |
| method | precise | retain | target |
| minor | predict | revenue | task |
| modify | previous | role | technical |
| monitor | primary | | technique |
| | prime | **S** | technology |
| **N** | principal | scheme | text |
| negate | principle | section | theory |
| network | prior | sector | tradition |
| normal | proceed | secure | transfer |
| notion | process | seek | transit |
| | professional | select | trend |
| **O** | project | sequence | |
| objective | promote | series | **U** |
| obtain | proportion | sex | undertake |
| obvious | psychology | shift | |
| occupy | publish | significant | **V** |
| occur | purchase | similar | valid |
| option | pursue | site | vary |
| orient | | source | version |
| outcome | | specific | volume |
| output | **R** | specify | |
| overall | range | stable | **W** |
| | ratio | statistic | welfare |
| | react | status | whereas |
| **P** | regime | strategy | |
| parallel | region | stress | |
| parameter | register | structure | |
| participate | regulate | | |

*Source:* Adapted from A. Coxhead, "A New Academic Word List," *TESOL Quarterly* 34, no. 2 (2000): 213–38.

### EXAMPLE

A. *occupy* (verb): to be, live, or work in a place.

That company is very large. Its offices <u>occupy</u> three city blocks.

*occupation* (noun): job or profession

Teaching is his <u>occupation</u>.

B. *cóntrast* (noun): a comparison between two things that shows a difference.

Although they are brothers, most people think they are from different families. The <u>contrast</u> in how they look, talk, and dress is amazing.

*contrást* (verb): to differ; to analyze the differences.

The speaker was very interesting. She was <u>contrasting</u> life in the United States with life in Peru.

3. Once you feel comfortable with the meaning and use of a word in your new word pile, put this card into a second group, which we will call the **review pile,** and then make another card for a new word from table 1.1. Add this card to your new word pile.

4. Once a week, repeat step 2.

5. As you read and come across other new words you (or your teacher) think you should learn, make flash cards for them, too, and add them to your new word pile.

6. Try to learn at least 25 new words per week. You should probably have no more than 50 words in your new word pile at a time.

7. Review the words in your review pile once a week or so. If you have trouble remembering a word or how it is used, put it back in your new word pile. Your goal is to be able to *automatically* recognize the words and know how they are used without having to stop and think about them.

## Explanation and Examples

Even after you learn all of the academic words in table 1.1, when you read a textbook you will still encounter many words that you have not yet learned. When you find a word you don't know, it is important to have strategies to help figure out its meaning.

First, decide whether or not you have to know the meaning of the word. If the purpose is only to get a general idea of the text, you can probably skip over some unknown words, especially if they are not **key words.** Consider skipping over the word if

- the unknown word is an adjective or an adverb.
- you can get the general idea of the sentence without knowing the word.

If an unknown word is repeated several times, or if it is clear that it is a key word that is important to know in order to understand the text, try these three strategies:

1. Use the context surrounding the word to guess the meaning.
2. Analyze the parts of the word to guess the meaning.
3. Use a dictionary to look up the exact meaning.

Since you will want to avoid looking up every word you don't know in a dictionary and analyzing word parts is not always easy to do, let's focus on how to use context to guess the meaning of a word.[3]

## Procedures for Guessing Meaning from Context

A. Look at the unknown word and decide its part of speech.

- Is it a noun, a verb, an adjective, or an adverb?

B. Look at the clause or sentence containing the unknown word.

- If the unknown word is a noun, what adjectives describe it? What verb is near it? That is, what does this noun do, and what is done to it?

- If the unknown word is a verb, what noun does it go with? Is it modified by an adverb?

- If it is an adjective, what noun does it go with?

- If it is an adverb, what verb is it modifying?

C. Look at the relationship between the sentence containing the unknown word and other sentences.

- For example, is there a contrast, or an effect, being described? Sometimes this relationship will be signaled by a conjunction like *but, because, if, when,* or by an adverb like *however* or *as a result.* Often there will be no signal.

- See chapter 4 for the types of relationships to look for and the many ways these relationships can be signaled.

D. Use the knowledge you have gained from these procedures to guess the meaning of the word.

E. Check that your guess is correct.

- See that the part of speech of your guess is the same as the part of speech of the unknown word and that your guess can replace it in the sentence. If your guess cannot replace the unknown word, then something is wrong with your guess.

- Replace the unknown word with your guess. If the sentence makes sense, your guess is probably correct.

Remember, you won't always be able to guess the meaning of a word from context using these procedures, but oftentimes you can.

---

3. The steps that follow are adapted from I. S. P. Nation, *Teaching and Learning Vocabulary* (New York: Newbury House, 1990). They can also be found in I. S. P. Nation, *Learning Vocabulary in Another Language* (Cambridge: Cambridge University Press, 2001).

**Activity** ➔ Each of the following paragraphs has an underlined word (or word family) that you probably do not know. For each unknown word, complete steps A–E described above to help you guess its meaning; then look the word up in the dictionary to see how accurate your guess is (was it perfect? or was it pretty close or way off?).

*EXAMPLE*

Written messages also vary in formality. At one extreme are the scribbled notes that people use to jog their own memories; at the other extreme are elaborate, formal reports that <u>rival</u> magazines in graphic quality. (Thill and Bovée 1993, 60)

A.  **Part of speech:** <u>rival</u> is a verb.

B.  **Context:** Formal <u>reports rival magazines</u> in graphic quality.

C.  **Relationship:** "at one extreme" and "at the other extreme" show that a contrast is being made between <u>scribbled notes</u> and <u>formal reports that rival magazines in graphic quality</u>.

D.  **Guess:** Scribbled notes look very messy and formal reports look very neat and professional. Magazines are very neat and professional, too, so <u>rival</u> probably means "compare with" or "are like" since both are being contrasted with scribbled notes.

E.  **Check:** Both "compare with" and "are like" can replace "rival" in the sentence. "Formal reports <u>compare with</u> magazines in graphic quality." "Formal reports <u>are like</u> magazines in graphic quality." Both sentences seem to make sense.

**Dictionary Definition:** (verb) to be as good as, be similar to

**Accuracy:** Perfect

1. It's also a good idea to try to think of information needs that your audience may not even be aware of. For example, suppose that your company has just hired a new employee from out of town and that you've been assigned to coordinate the person's <u>relocation</u>. At a minimum, you would write a welcoming letter describing your company's procedures for <u>relocating</u> employees. But with a little extra thought, you might decide to include some information about the city. . . . (Thill and Bovée 1993, 54)

   A.  **Part of speech:**

   B.  **Context:**

   C.  **Relationship:**

**D. Guess:**

**E. Check:**

**Dictionary definition:** _____

**Accuracy:** _____

2. The concept of temperature is based upon human <u>sensations</u> of "hotness" and "coldness." You can judge whether one object is hotter or colder than another by touching them. A hotter object is said to be at a higher temperature. (Dorin, Demmin, and Gabel 1992, 92)

   **A. Part of speech:**

   **B. Context:**

   **C. Relationship:**

   **D. Guess:**

   **E. Check:**

**Dictionary definition:** _____

**Accuracy:** _____

3. Culture is <u>transmitted</u> in society. Don't we learn our culture by observing, listening, talking, and interacting with many other people? Shared beliefs, values, memories, and expectations link people who grow up in the same culture. (Kottack 2000, 62)

    **A. Part of speech:**

    **B. Context:**

    **C. Relationship:**

    **D. Guess:**

    **E. Check:**

    **Dictionary definition:** _____

    **Accuracy:** _____

The following paragraphs, taken from the chapter in appendix 1 on ecosystems, have four underlined words that you may not know (the first word is used twice). For each of these underlined words, complete the five steps described above to help guess meaning from the context.

4. The basic building blocks of all **matter** (all gases, liquids, and solids in both living and nonliving systems) are **atoms.** Only 92 different kinds of atoms occur in nature, and these are known as the 92 naturally occurring **elements.** . . .

    How can the <u>innumerable</u> materials that make up our world, including the tissues of living things, be made up of just 92 elements? More specifically, 99% of Earth's crust is <u>composed</u> of only eight of these natural elements.

    Elements are <u>analogous</u> to Lego® blocks: From a small number of basic kinds of blocks, we can build <u>innumerable</u> different things. Also, like blocks, nature's materials can be taken apart into their separate <u>constituent</u> atoms, and the atoms can then be reassembled into different materials. (Nebel and Wright 1998, 52)

## Putting It into Practice

**Part 1.** Read through the first few pages of the textbook chapter in appendix 1 titled "Ecosystems: How They Work." Locate at least ten nontechnical words that you do not know and write the sentences in which they appear on a separate sheet of paper. (Technical words are words that a textbook introduces and defines within the text. These are discussed in chapter 2.) Circle each unknown word. For each unknown word, complete the five steps A–E described above. Check the meaning in a dictionary to see how accurate your guess is.

**Part 2.** Using a textbook that you are reading for an academic class, other materials assigned by your instructor, or the textbook chapter in appendix 2 titled "The Diffusion of Languages," read the first few pages of one chapter and locate at least ten nontechnical words that you do not know. Write the sentences in which they appear on a separate sheet of paper. Circle each unknown term. For each unknown word, complete the five steps described above for guessing meaning from context. Check the meaning in a dictionary to see how accurate your guess is.

# Chapter 2 RECOGNIZING TECHNICAL TERMS DEFINED IN CONTEXT

Most academic texts introduce and define many *technical terms;* these are terms the authors do not expect the reader to know already. Many of these technical terms are clearly defined in the text, but many are defined in less obvious ways. This chapter highlights the variety of ways that technical terms can be defined in academic texts.

## Explanation and Examples

1. **Parentheses:** Parentheses can be used to define technical terms in two ways.

   A. In the first way, the definition or explanation of the word is enclosed in parentheses immediately after the technical term. The following is an example.

   1a. In order to produce the majority of sounds in the world's languages, we take air into the lungs and then expel it during speech. A certain level of air pressure is needed to keep the speech mechanism functioning steadily. The pressure is maintained by the action of various sets of muscles coming into play during the course of an utterance. The muscles are primarily the **intercostals** (the muscles between the ribs) and the **diaphragm** (the large sheet of muscle separating the chest cavity from the abdomen). (O'Grady, Dobrovolsky, and Aronoff 1997, 18)

In this example two technical terms are introduced, *intercostals* and *diaphragm,* and both are defined by a phrase enclosed in parentheses that immediately follows them. Intercostals are "the muscles between the ribs," and the diaphragm is "the large sheet of muscle separating the chest cavity from the abdomen."

B.  The second way that parentheses can be used is with the technical term itself enclosed in parentheses following the introduction of the concept. The following is an example.

1b.  Phonetics is concerned with how speech sounds are produced (articulated) in the vocal tract (a field of study known as *articulatory phonetics*), as well as with the physical properties of the speech sound waves generated by the vocal tract (a field known as *acoustic phonetics*). (Akmajian et al. 1995, 59)

In this example, the three technical terms that are introduced—*articulated, articulatory phonetics,* and *acoustic phonetics*—are given inside the parentheses after the general definition is presented. *Articulated* refers to how the speech sounds are produced; *articulatory phonetics* is the study of how speech sounds are produced; and *acoustic phonetics* is the study of the physical properties of sound waves generated by the vocal tract.

2. **Bold or Italics:** Academic texts often set off technical words by using either bold or italics. This use of bold and italics can be seen in the above two examples. Two more examples are given below.

2a.  When the vocal folds are brought close together, but not tightly closed, air passing between them causes them to vibrate, producing sounds that are said to be **voiced.** (O'Grady, Dobrovolsky, and Aronoff 1997, 18)

2b.  In Anderson's view, *declarative knowledge* refers to facts and beliefs that we have about the world. (Glover and Bruning 1987, 81)

In these two examples, the texts are signaling the technical terms that are being defined in the sentences, **voiced** and *declarative knowledge,* by using bold or italic print. Using this visual clue, the reader is able to recognize easily the introduction and definition of a new technical term. **Voiced** describes the sounds that are made when the vocal folds vibrate; *declarative knowledge* is the facts and beliefs that we have about the world.

3. **"Defining" Verbs:** Many verbs, just by their presence, often indicate that a definition is being given. These verbs, and verb phrases, include the following: *to refer to, to be, to consist of, to be called,* and *to be defined as.*

3a.  **AIDS (acquired immune deficiency syndrome)** is a viral disease that reduces the immune system's ability to defend against the introduction of foreign substances (antigens). (Rings and Kremer 2000, 596)

In example 3a, we know to look for a definition of *AIDS* because the term is followed by *is*. A technical term followed by a present tense form of the verb *to be* (*is, are*) usually indicates a definition is being given. (Note also that a definition is given for the technical term *antigens*, which is the last word in parentheses. The definition for *antigens* immediately precedes it: *foreign substances.* See point 1b above.)

3b.  The standard deviation(*s*) is defined as the positive square root of the variance. (Howell 1987, 40)

In example 3b, we are informed that a definition of *standard deviation* is being given, as this technical term is immediately followed by the verb phrase *is defined as.*

3c. **Episodic memory** refers to memory for autobiographical events, including the context (time, place, setting) in which they occurred. (Medin and Ross 1992, 231)

In example 3c, not only is the technical term in bold type, but the text tells us a definition follows by using the verb phrase *refers to.*

3d. Chemists use abbreviations for the names of the elements. These abbreviations are called **chemical symbols.** (Dorin, Demmin, and Gabel 1992, 79)

In example 3d, the technical term *chemical symbols* is in bold and follows the verb phrase *are called,* which tells us that "abbreviations for the names of the elements" is the definition of *chemical symbols.*

Although each of the above examples demonstrates a different form, each functions to define the technical term that is being introduced.

4. **Appositives:** An appositive is a group of words (often starting with the word *which* or *that*) separated from the rest of the sentence by a comma, or sometimes dashes (—), that defines or clarifies a word or concept. These can be a little more difficult to spot but are important structures that good readers learn to look for.

4a. This difference is an example of the typicality effect, which occurs when instances that are more typical of a category are recognized more quickly than [unusual] instances of that category. (Medin and Ross 1992, 221)

In example 4a, *typicality effect* is defined by the whole clause immediately following it that is introduced by *which,* preceded by a comma.

5. **Restatements ("that is, . . .", "i.e., . . .", "or"):** Many textbooks give a technical term or concept and then provide a clarifying explanation, restating the term's meaning using other words. These restatements are often introduced by the phrase *that is* or the equivalent abbreviation, *i.e.* (*i.e.* is an abbreviation for the Latin phrase *id est,* which means *that is*), or the word *or.*

5a. This case illustrates **retroactive interference;** that is, later learning interferes with the recall of prior learning. (Glover and Bruning 1987, 56)

5b. The resulting phrases are what traditional grammarians refer to as appositives, i.e., a group of words following an expression which further defines that expression. (Celce-Murcia and Larsen-Freeman 1983, 381)

In example 5a, *that is* introduces a clause that explains what the technical term "retroactive interference" means. In example 5b, *i.e.* introduces an explanation of the technical term *appositives.*

The word *or* can be used in a similar way.

5c. In nature, **anaerobic,** or *oxygen-free,* environments commonly exist in the sediment at the bottom of marshes or swamps, buried deep in the earth, and in the guts of animals where oxygen does not penetrate readily. (Nebel and Wright 1998, 66)

As with the phrase *that is, . . .* or *i.e., . . .,* the word *or* in the sentence above introduces a clarification/definition of the technical term *anaerobic,* which means "oxygen-free."

6. **Delayed Definitions:** Sometimes a technical term is introduced in one sentence, but the definition for the term is given in another sentence, usually the next one. These, too, can be difficult to see, but it is important to learn to recognize them.

6a. The natural communication systems of other primates (monkeys and apes) are **call systems.** These vocal systems consist of a limited number of sounds —*calls*—that are produced only when particular environmental stimuli are encountered. (Kottack 2000, 82)

In this example, the technical term, *call systems,* is introduced in the first sentence, but its definition is delayed and given in the second sentence. It is important to see this connection between the two sentences in order to understand what *call systems* really are.

**Activity** → For each of the following sentences and short paragraphs, circle the technical term(s) or concept(s) that is (are) being defined and then underline the definition(s). In the blank that follows, write the textual clues that identify the technical term(s) and definition(s).

*EXAMPLE*

(Declarative memory) refers to memory for facts such as knowing that Des Moines is the capital of Iowa or that you ate spaghetti for dinner last night.

Clues: ___(a) "Declarative memory" is in bold.___

_____(b) the verb phrase "refers to" indicates that a definition is being given.___

_____

1. In contrast to the primary group, the **secondary group** is *a large and impersonal social group whose members pursue a specific interest or activity.* (Macionis 1997, 175)

Clues: _____

2. The cell body collects information from the **dendrites**—small branched extensions that spread out from the cell body. (Miller and Levine 1998b, 21)

Clues: _____

3. Opposing ethnocentrism is cultural relativism, the argument that behavior in one culture should not be judged by the standards of another culture. (Kottack 2000, 70)

Clues: _____

4. These talks with Nobel laureates were semi-structured interviews—that is, the general and specific issues to be covered were worked out in advance but the subjects were free to talk about each topic in the terms most meaningful to them. In contrast, structured interviews are ones in which the wording and sequence of questions are carefully planned in advance. In an unstructured interview, the questions and topics are not predetermined and the interviewer and the subject engage in free-flowing conversation. (Macionis 1997, 40)

> **Note:** In the above example, see if you can recognize another way for technical terms to be introduced and defined that was not discussed.

Clues: _____

5. Hydrologists (water experts) estimate that water shortages place a severe constraint on food production, economic development, and protection of natural ecosystems as available water drops below about 1000 cubic meters per year. (Nebel and Wright 1998, 264)

Clues: _____

6. As precipitation hits the ground, it may follow either of two pathways. It may soak into the ground, **infiltration,** or it may run off the surface, **runoff.** . . . Runoff flows over the ground surface into streams and rivers, which make their way to the ocean or inland seas. All the land area that contributes water to a particular stream or river is referred to as the **watershed** for that stream or river. (Nebel and Wright 1998, 267)

Clues: _____

7. Koko and the chimps also show that apes share still another linguistic ability with humans—**productivity.** Speakers routinely use the rules of their language to produce entirely new expressions that are comprehensible to other native speakers. (Kottack 2000, 83)

Clues: _____

8. Every status carries with it a socially prescribed role—that is, a set of expected behaviors, attitudes, obligations, and privileges. (Macionis 1997, 56)

Clues: _____

9. The term **desertification** has come into use since the 1960s to refer to the expansion of desert conditions into areas that previously were not deserts. (Bergman 1995, 72)

Clues: _____

10. If you had no concern for future jobs or income, there would be little point in doing homework now. You might as well party all day if you're that present-oriented. On the other hand, if you value future jobs and income, it makes sense to allocate some present time to studying. Then you'll have more human capital (knowledge and skills) later to pursue job opportunities. (Schiller 2002, 11)

Clues: _____

## Putting It into Practice  ▌▐ ▌

**Part 1.** The textbook chapter in appendix 1, "Ecosystems: How They Work," uses all six ways of identifying and explaining technical terms that are described above. Scan through this chapter and find <u>at least one example of each of these six ways</u> in which the definition of technical terms is given in academic texts. Not all technical terms are marked by bold or italics, so some may be more difficult to spot than others. Write out the sentences containing each technical term on a separate sheet of paper. Circle the technical term and underline the definition that the text provides. Write the textual clues that tell you what the technical terms and definitions are.

**Part 2.** Using a textbook that you are reading for an academic class, other materials assigned by your instructor, or the textbook chapter in appendix 2 titled "The Diffusion of Languages," scan through several pages and find at least five more examples of technical words or concepts that are defined in the text. Locate an example of at least three of the six types of clues textbooks often use to mark the location and definition of technical terms, as discussed above. If you can find an example of all six ways, that's even better! Write the sentences in which the technical words appear on a separate sheet of paper. Circle the technical term and underline the definition that the text provides. Write the textual clues that tell you what the technical terms and definitions are.

# Chapter 3 PRONOUNS AND RESTATEMENTS: IDENTIFYING CONTINUING IDEAS

Pronouns and other forms of restatements are frequently used to represent ideas that have already been introduced in the text. A single pronoun can represent an idea that is one word, a sentence, or even several paragraphs long. An important key to effectively reading academic texts is understanding the relationship between previously mentioned ideas and the pronouns and restatements that refer to them.

In many cases, it is easy to see the relationship between the restatement and the original idea. You have no trouble understanding sentences like the following.

1. I found a great new restaurant. *It* serves both Chinese and Vietnamese food.
2. West Germany and East Germany used to be two separate countries. *They* have now combined into one country, Germany.

In the first example, *it* refers back to the idea "a great new restaurant." In the second example, *they* refers back to "West Germany and East Germany."

The use of third-person pronouns (*he, she, it, they*) is probably the most common way of restating a previously mentioned idea. However, there are a variety of other techniques that writers frequently use to restate ideas.

## Explanation and Examples

1. *This, That, These,* or *Those:* All of these words can replace nouns, or they can replace a group of words or sentences when they are referring to a particular fact or idea.

    1a. Varen differentiated two approaches to geography. One he called "special geography." *This* was the description and analysis of any place in each of ten categories: (1) "the stature of the natives"; (2) employment; (3) . . . (Bergman 1995, 3)

In this context, *this* is referring back to the previously stated idea "special geography," which is the first of two approaches to geography that Varen is describing.

2. *The/This/That/These/Those* + **(previously mentioned noun):** Frequently, a previously mentioned noun that has been identified is restated using this structure.

   2a. A great part of the world's land area is cultivated or pastured. In *this* huge *area,* the visible imprint of humankind might best be called the **agricultural landscape.** (Jordan-Bychkov and Domosh 1999, 126)

*This area* is referring back to the great part of the world's land area that is cultivated or pastured.

3. *The/This/That/These/Those* + **(new noun):** A previously mentioned idea is often restated using a synonym. If the idea is a verb, an adjective, or an adverb, the noun form of these words is often used.

   3a. Other research has examined how less integrated aspects of the learning and retrieval context may affect memory. *This work* has distinguished between two types of context clues, external cues such as the physical environment and internal cues such as body states. (Medin and Ross 1992, 190)

In this example, *work* is a synonym for "research" and refers to the "other research" that has examined how less integrated aspects of the learning and retrieval context may affect memory.

   3b. Becoming wealthy by winning the lottery is the dream of many. *That* unearned *wealth,* however, often brings with it many problems.

Here, *that wealth* is a noun that carries on the idea expressed previously by the adjective *wealthy.*

4. *The/This/That/These/Those* + **(general word/phrase):** When an idea is being referred back to, it is frequently restated using *the/this/that/these/those* plus a general word or phrase that summarizes the idea.

   4a. All cognitive processes are invisible. *This fact,* though obvious, implies a basic difficulty in the study of cognitive processes. (Glover and Bruning 1987, 22)

5. *Such (a)* + **(general word/phrase):** Using *such (a)* + general word/phrase is another structure that writers use to refer back to a previously stated idea, with the general word or phrase being directly related to, but less specific than, the original idea.

   5a. Closely related to the concept of the folk fortress is the distribution of terrain. Ideally, a country should have mountains and hills around its edges and plains in the interior. *Such a pattern* not only facilitates defense but also provides a natural unit of enclosed plains as the basis for a cohesive country. (Jordan-Bychkov and Domosh 1999, 158)

*Such a pattern* refers back to the pattern of having mountains and hills around a country's edges and plains in its interior.

> **Note:** The five ways of restating ideas described above are not the only methods textbooks use, but they are the most common. As you read, look for other ways authors restate ideas.

**Activity →** Each of the following passages expresses an idea that is continued later on in the passage. Underline the restated idea and then write out the complete idea that this restatement refers back to. (Ignore the pronouns *he/she/it/they*.)

*EXAMPLE*

Most of the water used in homes and industries is for washing and flushing away undesired materials, and the water used in electrical power production is used for taking away waste heat. <u>Such uses</u> are termed **non-consumptive.** (Nebel and Wright 1998, 273)

Idea referred to:  Water used in homes and industries and in electrical

power production.

1. Religion can also influence the way people perceive their physical environment. Nowhere is this more evident than in the perception of environmental hazards such as floods, storms, and droughts. (Jordan-Bychkov and Domosh 1999, 240)

Idea referred to: _____

2. Have you ever awakened during the night and, just for a moment, been uncertain about where you were? Such temporary disruptions in our normal cognitive functioning are far from rare; many persons experience them from time to time as a result of fatigue, illness, or the use of alcohol or other drugs. (Rings and Kremer 2000, 633)

Idea referred to: _____

3. One of the common reasons given for dress is protection from inclement weather. Humans lack the body hair that protects other primates from the elements, so they depend on clothes and houses to create artificial environments for their bodies. These, in turn, enable them to survive almost everywhere on the earth, as well as in the sea and outer space. (Hiebert 1983, 79)

Idea referred to: _____

4. Perception of the physical environment plays a role when a group of people choose where to settle and live. In the European Alps, German-speaking people, who rely on dairy farming, long ago established permanent settlements some 650 feet (200 meters) higher on the shady slopes than the settlements of Italians, who are culturally tied to warmth-loving crops, on the sunny slopes. This example demonstrates contrasting cultural attitudes toward land use and different perceptions of the best use for one type of physical environment. (Jordan-Bychkov and Domosh 1999, 66)

Idea referred to: _____

5. The Amish rely much less on inanimate power and agricultural machines than does the average American farmer. A study comparing Amish and non-Amish farmers in three states—Pennsylvania, Illinois, and Wisconsin—not only revealed these fundamental differences in the farming practices but suggested that the Amish surpassed other agriculturists in the amount of food calories produced per unit of energy expended in the production process. (Jordan-Bychkov and Domosh 1999, 117)

Idea referred to: _____

6. No test bench is complete without a digital multimeter (DMM). This instrument is used for measuring dc and ac voltage, dc and ac current, and resistance. (Floyd 2000, 29)

Idea referred to: _____

## Putting It into Practice ▌ ▌ ▌

**Part 1.** Read through the first five pages (pp. 51–55) of the textbook chapter in appendix 1, "Ecosystems: How They Work." Locate as many examples of restatements as you can (at least ten). On a separate sheet of paper, write down all of the sentences that use restatements, including the page number on which you found them. For each sentence, underline the restatement and then indicate the idea that it is referring back to.

**Part 2.** Using a textbook that you are reading for an academic class, other materials assigned by your instructor, or the textbook chapter in appendix 2 titled "The Diffusion of Languages," scan through several pages of one chapter. Locate at least one example of at least three of the five types of restatements discussed above. Try to find examples of all five types if you can. Write your examples on a separate sheet of paper. Underline the restated idea and then indicate the idea to which it is referring.

# Part 2
## UNDERSTANDING EXPOSITORY TEXT STRUCTURES

Part 1 focused on improving your reading skills at the word level. While it is critical to be able to recognize words and how they are being used, to become a good reader you must also be able to quickly recognize how sentences and paragraphs are organized and how ideas are developed. The chapters in part 2 describe the ways academic texts are usually organized and what clues to look for to help you identify a text's organization.

Chapter 4 introduces many of the ways that relationships between ideas in a text are indicated and gives practice in looking for and identifying these relationships.

Chapter 5 provides an introduction to how paragraphs and groups of paragraphs are organized around one main idea. This chapter will help you learn to look for and identify these main ideas, which will help you better understand the information presented in textbooks.

Chapters 6–10 focus on the many different ways that textbooks organize information. The key features of these different structures will be given, and you will practice recognizing these structures in authentic texts.

# Chapter 4 LOGICAL CONNECTORS: RECOGNIZING DEVELOPMENT OF IDEAS

Most texts, especially ones that are well written, provide many cues—or markers—to indicate how the writer plans to develop or change the topic. These markers provide coherence to a text; in other words, they help make the connection from one idea to the next smoother. This chapter will look at a variety of connectors writers use and how they can help you follow the ideas that writers present.

## Explanation and Examples

Logical connectors can show the relationship of ideas within a sentence, between sentences in the same paragraph, or between paragraphs in a longer text. There are four basic types of logical connectors:

1. sentence conjunctions;
2. coordinating conjunctions;
3. subordinating conjunctions;
4. prepositions.

(A conjunction is simply a word that connects other words together.)

1. **Sentence Conjunctions:** Sentence conjunctions show the relationship between two independent clauses. These conjunctions generally occur between the clauses they connect.

   1a. *I wanted to buy my wife a ring.* **However,** *I couldn't find one I liked.* (The word "however" shows that a contrast is being made between the first sentence and the second.)

   1b. *Bob was very surprised he didn't pass the test;* **in fact,** *he is quite upset.* (The words "in fact" indicate that additional information is being added to clarify the previous sentence.)

2. **Coordinating Conjunctions:** These connectors join two structures that are similar, or coordinated. For example, the coordinating conjunction *and* can connect

    2a. two noun phrases— *"John's mother* **and** *Bob's sister* are at the store."

    2b. two prepositional phrases— *"As predicted* **and** *as demonstrated,* water and oil don't mix."

    2c. two independent clauses— *"I had a wonderful vacation,* **and** *I am so glad that I could go."*

3. **Subordinating Conjunctions:** The verb *to subordinate* means to put into a lower or inferior class. That is what a subordinating conjunction does. It makes an independent clause (which can stand by itself) into a dependent clause (which must be connected to an independent clause). In the examples that follow, dependent clauses are underlined once, and independent clauses are underlined twice.

    3a. <u>While she was at the store</u>, <u><u>Naomi saw her best friend</u></u>.
           ↑    (dependent clause)      (independent clause)
     (subordinating conjunction)

    (The dependent clause that starts with the subordinating conjunction *while* indicates **when** Naomi saw her friend.)

    3b. <u><u>I was late to the meeting</u></u> <u>because I couldn't find the directions to the office</u>.
       (independent clause)      ↑         (dependent clause)
           (subordinating conjunction)

    (The dependent clause that starts with the subordinating conjunction *because* indicates **why** I was late to the meeting.)

4. **Prepositions:** Many prepositions, which are always followed by a noun or noun phrase, also help to show the logical structure of ideas in a sentence. The ideas connected by prepositions usually occur within the same sentence.

    4a. *Like Bob,* I don't plan to see the movie *Titanic.* (The preposition *like* shows similarity.)

    4b. *Despite my efforts to stop him,* Larry quit his job and moved away. (The preposition *despite* shows contrast—my efforts to make Larry change his mind did not work.)

It is important to watch for these four different types of logical connectors because they provide important information about the relationship between ideas presented in the text. In fact, many writers purposely use these different connectors to help readers understand how the ideas are organized and the relationship between them. Table 4.1 lists most of the connectors used in academic textbooks. The first column of table 4.1 indicates the type of relationship that connectors typically show between two ideas. The other columns in table 4.1 give examples that signal this type of relationship for each of the four classes of connectors.

**TABLE 4.1. Types of Logical Connectors and the Relationships They Indicate**

| Relationship Indicated by Connectors | Sentence Conjunctions | Coordinating Conjunctions | Subordinating Conjunctions | Prepositions |
|---|---|---|---|---|
| **TIME** Provides *time* information—when one event occurred relative to another | I walked into the room alone. **Subsequently,** the door slammed shut behind me. **Meanwhile,** all my friends were at a party upstairs. **Eventually,** my friends wondered where I was and came looking for me. OTHERS: at present, now, (at) first, first of all, originally, to start with, then, next, after that, later, finally, lastly, in the end, at last, so far | | **By the time** (that) I realized I was alone, I had already walked into the room. **As** I walked into the room, the door slammed shut. **At the time** the door slammed shut, I was by myself. **Since** the day the door slammed shut, I've been scared to go in there by myself. **Once** I understood how frightened I was, I decided to see a counselor. OTHERS: when, while, after, before, during, until, as soon as, as/so long as, whenever, now that, every time (that), up to the time (that) | I was never afraid of anything **before** this happened to me. **After** this event, I have never gone into a room alone. **Within** five minutes, my life changed forever. OTHERS: during, up to, since, until, from, by, for, etc. |
| **CONDITION** Provides *conditional* information—the condition under which the event takes place or will take place (which may only be hypothetical) | I hope they will offer me more money. **Otherwise,** I will not accept the position. | I want to make $75,000 dollars per year at this job, **or (else)** I will not accept it. **Either** I get the salary I want **or** I will look for another position. | **Even if** I am having trouble finding another job, I don't want that one. **Provided (that)** I can make the salary I want, I will work there. **Whether or not** I get the job, I'm glad I went to the interview. **Whether** I get this job or another job, I will be happy. **If** I get it, **(then)** I will be happy. OTHERS: unless, in case | **In case of** bad luck, I will bring my good luck charm with me to the interview. I know I will do well, **regardless of** my anxieties. |
| **ADDITION** Provides *additional* information—another point is being added. | I think the fair is a wonderful event. **Moreover,** I think we should help sponsor it by contributing $3,000. **As a matter of fact,** I have already sent in a check. I have promised to send the fair more money, **as well.** OTHERS: also, in addition, too, furthermore, besides, what is more, in fact, certainly, actually, above all, indeed | **Not only** are Bob and Sue going to the fair, **but also** Joe and Sally. Sam is not going to the fair, **and neither** is Jack. OTHERS: neither . . . nor, both . . . and, nor, and | **In addition to** going to the fair this week, we plan to go to the museum. **Besides** visiting the museum, we will also do some shopping, **not to mention** going out to eat. | **Besides** my contribution, I want to help other people contribute. **In addition to** other people, I want to see corporations contribute. |

**TABLE 4.1—Continued**

| Relationship Indicated by Connectors | Sentence Conjunctions | Coordinating Conjunctions | Subordinating Conjunctions | Prepositions |
|---|---|---|---|---|
| **EXAMPLE** Provides an *example* of an idea that has just been stated. | I like ethnic foods. **In particular,** I like to eat Chinese food. **As an example,** I've eaten Chinese food four times this week already. **OTHERS:** for example (e.g.), for instance, to illustrate | (Sentence punctuation will also signal examples.) I like ethnic foods—Chinese, Italian, Japanese—more than fast foods (McDonald's, Burger King). **OTHERS:** : (colon) | | I like ethnic foods **such as** Chinese food. I don't like fast food, **like** Burger Biggie. |
| **CLARIFICATION** Provides *clarification* of an idea that has just been stated. | I'm concerned that Bill will not be able to do this. **In other words,** I don't think he is qualified. **OTHERS:** that is (i.e.) | (Sentence punctuation will also signal clarification of ideas.) Bill is qualified to do this job; he has a college degree. **OTHERS:** ( ) (parentheses), — (dash) , (comma) | | |
| **COMPARISON** Shows the *similarity* between two ideas. | The English language has borrowed a lot of words from French. **Similarly,** the Japanese language has borrowed a lot of its language from Chinese. **OTHERS:** in the same way, likewise | | **As much as** I enjoy Italian food, I like Thai food even better. | **Like** Japanese, the English language has borrowed many words from other languages. |
| **CONTRAST** Shows *alternatives, contrast* or *opposition* between two ideas. Or shows that certain events took place *contrary to our expectations.* | It would be a lot of fun to buy a car. **On the other hand,** taking the bus would be cheaper. My father wants me to save my money for college; **even so,** I want to buy a car. **Nevertheless,** I do need to save money for college if I want to get a good job. **In spite of this,** I need to have a car to get to my job. **Still,** I will do what my father asks. **OTHERS:** alternatively, nonetheless, however, on the other hand, in contrast, on the contrary, admittedly | You can buy a car, **or** you can take the bus. **Either** I buy a car, or I will have to quit my job. I want to buy a new car, **but** my dad said I should save my money for school. I really want to obey my dad, **yet** I need a way to get to work. | **Whereas** I have to walk to school every day, you can take a bus. **While** you have to take the bus, John can drive his new car. **Despite the fact that** I am 21 years old, I don't have my license. I'm going to buy a car, **regardless of** what anyone says. **OTHERS:** although, (even) though, in spite of the fact that, -er/more/less . . . than ("He is a faster driver **than** I am." "She is **more** patient **than** I am.") | **In contrast to** my friends, my father wants me to save money for college. **Unlike** my brother, I'd rather have a car than go to college. **OTHERS:** instead of, different from |

| | Transition | Coordinating | Subordinating | Prepositional |
|---|---|---|---|---|
| **CAUSE—REASON**<br>Shows *reason, cause,* or *purpose* for an idea | My mother's parents came here from Italy. **With this in mind,** we decided to visit Rome on our trip.<br>**OTHERS:** for this purpose | I wanted to travel to Europe, **for** my ancestors emigrated from Germany. | I wanted to travel to Germany, **as** the travel agent said it was a beautiful country. The trip was not enjoyable **in that** it was poorly planned. I decided to go to France **inasmuch as** I was already in Europe. **As long as** we are there, we should also go to Spain.<br>**OTHERS:** because, since, now that, in view of the fact that, due to the fact that, so that, in order that, in order to | **In view of** your bad grades, you will have to go to summer school.<br>**OTHERS:** as a result of, because of, on account of, due to, for |
| **EFFECT**<br>Shows *result* or *effect* of an idea | It is important to know how to play golf well if you are a businessperson. **Accordingly,** I knew I had to take golf lessons. I practiced very hard. **Consequently,** my game has improved.<br>**OTHERS:** as a result, therefore, thus, hence | I didn't know how to play golf, **so** I decided to take golf lessons. I knew I would have to practice every day, **or (else)** I would never be able to play with my boss. | | |
| **SEQUENCE**<br>Shows the *logical sequence* of ideas | I don't like going to a doctor. **To start with,** I am scared of needles. **In the second place,** I find their offices are always cold.<br>**OTHERS:** first (of all), in the first place, to begin with, next, then, secondly, finally, to conclude, lastly, in conclusion, eventually, soon, so far | He made an appointment, **and** he went to see his doctor. | He began to feel worse **after** he took the medicine. **When** he read the directions, he realized he took too many pills. He decided to see if he felt better **before** he called the doctor. | |
| **SUMMARY**<br>Shows a *summary* of ideas | I like to fly. I like to drive. I like trains. **All in all,** I like to travel more than anything else.<br>**OTHERS:** in summary, to summarize, overall, briefly, in short, as has been mentioned/said | | | |

. . . . . . . . . . . .

**Activity** ➜ **Part 1.** With the connectors used in the sentences as clues, select the best answer to indicate the kind of information that *will likely follow* each of the sentences below, and then explain why you think it will follow.

*EXAMPLE*

The football player did not block the defender very well at all. Moreover . . .

a. (the reason the football player didn't block the defender well)

(b.) (a second thing that was not done very well)

*Explanation:* _The sentence conjunction moreover is used to show that an_
_additional idea is going to be presented._

1. He bought a new car, but . . .

   a. (comment about a problem with the car or about the purchase of it)

   b. (a description of how it is similar to another car)

   *Explanation:* _____

   _____

2. Due to the fact that he was late, . . .

   a. (a comment about what happened as a consequence)

   b. (a comment about the differences between two things)

   *Explanation:* _____

   _____

3. Provided that he retires this year, . . .

   a. (the addition of a second idea similar to the first)

   b. (a statement that indicates the result of a condition (a requirement))

   *Explanation:* _____

   _____

4. I would enjoy going to Spain for two weeks; on the other hand, . . .

   a. (an alternative idea)

   b. (a clarification of the idea given)

   *Explanation:* _____

   _____

**Part 2:** Read the following section taken from a sociology textbook. Most of the connectors in this section are in bold. For the ones that are numbered, explain the relationship to other ideas each connector suggests. Use table 4.1 to help you. (*Note:* connectors underlined with wavy lines have more than one part.) The first one has been done for you.

**Whether** it occurs in the federal bureaucracy, in the corporate world, **or**[1] in universities, sexual harassment generally takes place in organizations in which the hierarchy of authority finds White males at the top **and**[2] in which women's work is valued less than men's. One survey of the private sector found that African American women were three times more likely than White women to experience sexual harassment. From a conflict perspective, it is not surprising that women **and** especially women of color[3] are most likely to become victims of sexual harassment. . . .

**While**[4] it is agreed that sexual harassment is widespread in the United States, it is **nevertheless**[5] clear that most victims do not report these abuses to proper authorities. **For example,**[6] in a survey of federal government employees conducted in 1988, only 5 percent of those who had been harassed stated that they had filed complaints. "It takes a lot of self-confidence to fight," suggests Catherine Broderick, a lawyer for the Securities and Exchange Commission (SEC) who won a sexual harassment complaint against the agency's Washington office. Broderick had refused her supervisor's advances **and** then had been repeatedly denied promotions. **After**[7] a nine-year legal battle, Broderick was victorious in court **and** won a promotion and years of back pay. **Still,**[8] her experience is a reminder that pursuing justice against those guilty of sexual harassment can be costly and draining.

**Even if**[9] the victim does have the will to fight, the process of making a sexual harassment complaint in the courts **or**[10] in most bureaucracies is slow and burdensome. In 1992, Evn Kemp, head of the federal Equal Employment Opportunity Commission (EEOC), admitted that a woman who has filed a complaint of sexual harassment may have to wait as long as *four years* to get a hearing before the EEOC. The agency has a huge caseload;[11] it receives 60,000 complaints of discrimination each year **and also**[12] oversees 50,000 others that are handled by state fair-employment agencies. **Yet**[13] EEOC's funding is clearly inadequate to investigate all these cases.

Money, **however,**[14] is not the only problem. In many organizations, written procedures for handling complaints of sexual harassment lead to goal displacement by those in positions of power. (Schaefer and Lamm 1995, 168)

1. **Whether. . .or** indicates that any of the conditions ("in the federal bureaucracy, in the corporate world, or in universities") will lead to the same result (sexual harassment).

2. **and**

3. — . . . —

4. While

5. nevertheless

6. For example

7. After

8. Still

9. Even if

10. or

11. ;

12. and also

13. Yet

14. however

## Putting It into Practice

**Part 1.** Read again the first two pages of the textbook chapter in appendix 1, "Ecosystems: How They Work." Several different **types** of logical connectors are used in these two pages. Try to find and identify six *different* types of logical connector relationships (e.g., similarity, contrast) that are used. (See table 4.1.) Note that there are multiple examples of some of the different types. On a separate sheet of paper, write the sentences that the connectors occur in, underline the connectors, and indicate the relationship between ideas that each connector expresses. See if you can find any examples of logical connectors—and identify the relationship they indicate—that are not included in table 4.1.

**Part 2.** Using a textbook that you are reading for an academic class, other materials assigned by your instructor, or the textbook chapter in appendix 2 titled "The Diffusion of Languages," pick five consecutive paragraphs and analyze the use of logical connectors. Rewrite or photocopy the paragraphs, and then underline all the uses of logical connectors. For each, indicate the relationship that the logical connector indicates between two or more ideas.

# Chapter 5 DETERMINING MAIN IDEAS

Whenever you read something, the first question you should ask is, "Who or what is this about?" Often the title of the article or chapter or headings and subheadings in a textbook answer that question for you. For example, what is *this* chapter about? By looking at the title, you can see that the topic is how to determine main ideas when you read. Once you know the topic, the next question you should ask yourself is, "What does the author want me to know about this topic?" When you can answer this question, you will know what the main idea of the material is that you are reading. The **main idea** is the key piece of information that the author wants you to understand.

This chapter will look at different strategies that can help you figure out what the main ideas are in a text.

## Explanation and Examples

There are several important reasons why you need to figure out what the main ideas of a text are.

1. When you are actively trying to understand the main ideas, you have a purpose for reading, which helps you focus and concentrate.

2. Because the information and details in texts are used to explain or support main ideas, you will be able to remember more if you know what ideas are being explained.

3. It is easier to take notes and to study when you can recognize the main ideas.

Fortunately, most authors want you to know what their main ideas are. In fact, textbooks are usually written so that the main ideas are clearly stated. As you probably know from your writing classes, good paragraphs usually have a topic sentence around which the whole paragraph is structured. It is in this topic sentence that the main idea of the paragraph is stated. The following paragraph is a good example.

> [1]There are three general types of neurons, distinguished by the directions in which they carry impulses. [2]The **sensory neurons** carry impulses from the sense organs to the brain and the spinal cord. [3]**Motor neurons** carry impulses in the opposite direction—from the brain or spinal cord to muscles or other organs. [4]**Interneurons** connect sensory and motor neurons, and carry impulses between them.
> (Miller and Levine 1998b, 22)

Let's look at each sentence in this paragraph.

1. The first sentence notes the three types of neurons and how they are distinguished.
2. The second sentence describes one type of neuron (*sensory neurons*).
3. The third sentence describes a second type of neuron (*motor neurons*).
4. The fourth sentence describes a third type of neuron (*interneurons*).

Now go back to the two questions:

1. What is this paragraph about? It's about neurons.

2. What is it that the authors want us to know about neurons? They want us to know the three types and how they differ. This information is given in the first sentence, which is the **main idea.**

**Activity →
1**

With a little practice, it is usually not too difficult to identify the **topic** of a passage (what the passage is about), **the main idea** (what the author wants us to know about the topic) and the **specific details that support and explain** the main idea.

The statements in each group below are connected to each other. One of the statements gives the topic, one gives the main idea, and two provide supporting information. For each group, identify which statement is the topic (**T**), which is the main idea (**M**), and which provide supporting information (**S**).

1. a. ＿＿ During mating season, the canary's song center expands, adding new nerve cells.
   b. ＿＿ Researchers have found that a canary's brain changes size depending on the season.
   c. ＿＿ In the winter, when the canaries are more quiet, the song center shrinks.
   d. ＿＿ Seasonal changes in the size of canary brains

2. a. ＿＿ Warmer temperatures would melt polar ice and glaciers, raising sea levels and flooding coastal regions.
   b. ＿＿ Concerns about global warming
   c. ＿＿ A rise in the average surface temperature of the earth could have catastrophic consequences.
   d. ＿＿ Weather patterns would be affected by changes in temperature, causing droughts or flooding in different areas of the world.

3. a. ___ The Native American influence on modern American culture
   b. ___ Many common foods, like squash and corn, were first developed by Native Americans.
   c. ___ Aspects of Native American culture can still be seen in American culture today.
   d. ___ Many names of states, cities, rivers, and lakes come from Native American origins.

## Explanation and Examples

As noted above, writers frequently provide topic sentences to inform the reader what main idea they are discussing. Topic sentences, with the main ideas, are often the first sentence of a paragraph, as illustrated in the example on page 35. However, writers also sometimes put the main idea in the middle of a paragraph or even at the end of a paragraph; sometimes they do not state the main idea explicitly, assuming it is clear from what was written. Furthermore, many ideas are so complex that the writer discusses them across many paragraphs. **Remember—to determine what the main idea is, ask yourself: What is the paragraph or section about, and what does the author want me to know about the topic? What is the one key idea that all the sentences in the paragraph or section explain or describe?**

**Main Ideas in the Middle of a Paragraph:** The example on page 35 is a paragraph in which the main idea is given in the first sentence. Sometimes the main idea is found in the middle of a paragraph. In this type of paragraph, the sentences that occur before the main idea usually serve to connect the idea back to the previous paragraph or to other ideas that came earlier, give background information on the topic, or raise the interest of the reader.

> [1]People share society—organized life in groups—with other animals, including baboons, wolves, and even ants. [2]Culture, however, is distinctly human. [3]Cultures are traditions and customs, transmitted through learning, that govern the beliefs and behavior of the people exposed to them. [4]Children learn such a tradition by growing up in a particular society, through a process called enculturation. [5]Cultural traditions include customs and opinions, developed over the generations, about proper and improper behavior. (Kottack 2000, 4)

What is this paragraph about? It's about culture. What does the author want us to know about culture? He wants us to know what culture is. If we look at the paragraph more closely, we can see that the main idea is actually expressed in the middle of this paragraph, in sentence 3.

The first sentence (1) in this paragraph notes that people and animals both have social characteristics. This is background information.

The second sentence (2) points out that only humans have culture. This is also background information.

The third sentence (3) is the main idea, defining what culture is.

The last two sentences (4 and 5) then provide detail, explaining how children acquire culture and what types of traditions make up culture.

**Implied Main Ideas:** While main ideas are frequently expressed in topic sentences, usually at the beginning of paragraphs but also in the middle or end, some paragraphs do not have explicitly stated topic sentences; they are **implied.** But if the paragraph is well written, the main idea should still be clear. To determine the main idea in a paragraph where it is implied, ask the same two questions:

What is this paragraph about?

What does the author want us to know about this topic?

> [1]In medieval Europe, children past infancy were not clearly distinguished from adults. [2]Almost as soon as they could walk and talk, they entered adult society, becoming helpers in the fields or apprentices in workshops. [3]Children even dressed like adults, for clothes were determined more by social class than age. [4]Not until the seventeenth century—as we can see from the paintings of the period—did children begin to dress in a manner different from that of adults. [5]It was during this same period that childhood was first identified as a distinct stage of life. (Popenoe 2000, 265)

What is this paragraph about? It's about historical changes in the way children are viewed as compared to adults. If we look at the information provided, we see that sentences 1–3 describe how children were viewed in medieval Europe. Children were seen as "little" adults. Sentences 4 and 5 contrast this with how children were viewed in the seventeenth century, when they were seen as different from adults.

The main idea is not clearly stated, but with this information we can determine the main idea that the author wants us to know: *The concept of childhood evolved over time in Europe.*

**Activity →
2**

The following paragraphs are taken from academic textbooks in a variety of fields. Each has a main idea that is either stated in the paragraph or strongly implied. First, determine the topic of the paragraph: What is this about? Then, write the sentence that states the main idea or topic of the paragraph; if the main idea is implied, write the main idea in your own sentence.

1. The human nervous system is similar to a complex telephone network in a large city. In a telephone network, telephone lines and wires connect homes, businesses, and schools through a central telephone switching station. The nervous system has connecting wires as well—the neurons. The nervous system itself works like the central switching station of the body. It receives, compares, and analyzes information, then sends messages and commands to the rest of the body. (Miller and Levine 1998b, 25)

   What is the topic? _____

   Main idea: _____

2. Health psychology and behavioral medicine have experienced tremendous growth since their beginnings in the early 1970s. Perhaps the most fundamental reason for the increased interest in health psychology and behavioral medicine is the dramatic shift observed in the leading causes of death during this century. In 1900, many of the leading causes of death in the United States could be traced to infectious diseases such as influenza and tuberculosis. However, the development of antibiotics and vaccines and improved sanitation practices have significantly reduced these health threats, at least in this country. (Rings and Kremer 2000, 570–71)

What is the topic? _____

Main idea: _____

3. In the centuries that followed the domestication of the dog, humans learned to domesticate goats, sheep, camels, horses, and other familiar animals. Humans also learned to make new and better weapons, thus becoming more efficient at hunting wild animals. These abilities undoubtedly helped human communities and civilizations to develop. (Miller and Levine 1998a, 113)

What is the topic? _____

Main idea: _____

4. Two-party systems are not without disadvantages, however. The most important is that a two-party system can stifle the views of minority groups. In the United States, the news media give a great deal of coverage to the Democratic and Republican candidates for President. Candidates from other, minor parties usually receive very little attention, even though they may have important ideas to contribute. (Saffell 1996, 146)

What is the topic? _____

Main idea: _____

5. In lower animals, where instincts rather than culture guide social life, the young can function independently at a very early age. Animal young treat the first moving object they see after birth as "mother"—a process called *imprinting*— but a baby duckling will follow its instincts to search out water and swim even if the first moving object it sees is a hen. Lacking instincts, an unprotected human infant would have less chance of survival than most newborn animals, but at the same time, animals' dependence on instincts limits them to a rigid set of behaviors. (Popenoe 2000, 115)

What is the topic? _____

Main idea: _____

## Explanation and Examples

Academic texts are seldom only one paragraph long, and much of the information that an author wants to give may be fairly complex. Consequently, writers frequently present their ideas in ways different from those we have already discussed. For example, the main idea for one paragraph may be given in another paragraph. Or one main idea may be developed across several paragraphs. Even in these situations, you can determine the main idea by asking the same two questions.

1. What is this about?
2. What does the author want me to know about this topic?

In the following example, the main idea is given in the first paragraph, but is then developed in the next several paragraphs. Read the paragraphs below, then answer these questions:

1. What is this about?
2. What is the main idea?
3. What is the support that the author gives to develop the main idea?

> How any organization performs depends not only on its internal structure but also on the **organizational environment,** *a range of factors external to an organization that affects its operation.* Such factors include technology, politics, population patterns, the economy, as well as other organizations.
>
> *Technology* is especially critical in the modern organizational environment. We have already noted that today's organizations could hardly exist without the communication links provided by telephone systems, facsimile (fax) machines and the ability to duplicate, process, and store information afforded by copiers and computers. . . .
>
> A second dimension of the organizational environment is *politics.* Changes in law often have dramatic consequences for the operation of an organization as many industries have learned in the face of new environmental standards imposed by government. (Macionis 1997, 194)

The topic for all three of these paragraphs is "organizational environment," and the main idea is how the organizational environment—external factors—affects an organization's operation; this is stated in the first sentence of the first paragraph. In the second paragraph, the main idea for this paragraph—the influence of technology—provides one example of the influence of the organizational environment; it is a supporting paragraph. In the third paragraph, the main idea for this paragraph—the influence of politics—provides another example of the influence of the organizational environment on an organization.

In fact, the second sentence of the first paragraph gives you a roadmap of what the next several paragraphs of this text will be discussing—the influence of population patterns, the economy, and other organizations on an organization's operation—all of which support the main idea given in the first paragraph. It's easy to see that all of these paragraphs must be read together in order to be understood.

## Putting It into Practice ▌▌▌

**Part 1a.** In the textbook chapter in appendix 1, "Ecosystems: How They Work," read the eight paragraphs of the section titled "Energy Considerations," which begins on page 55 and ends on page 59. For each of these paragraphs, write out the main idea for the paragraph and state where it is located (e.g., first sentence, last sentence, implied).

**Part 1b.** Find the section "Energy Laws: Laws of Thermodynamics," on page 59 in the textbook chapter in appendix 1, "Ecosystems: How They Work." Read the six paragraphs in this section; you will see that they all develop one general idea. After you have read the section, answer these questions.

1. What is the topic of these six paragraphs? [*Hint:* See the title for the section.]
2. What is the main idea? Where is it stated (or implied)? [*Hint:* It's not directly stated. Look at the heading title for this section and the last paragraph for clues.]
3. What is the support given to develop the main idea? Where is it given?

**Part 2a:** Using a textbook that you are reading for an academic class, other materials assigned by your instructor, or the textbook chapter in appendix 2 titled "The Diffusion of Languages," pick out **three** different paragraphs. Photocopy or write out each example. For each, answer these questions.

1. What is the paragraph about?
2. What is the main idea?
3. What is the support given to develop the main idea?

**Part 2b.** Using a textbook that you are reading for an academic class, other materials assigned by your instructor, or the textbook chapter in appendix 2 titled "The Diffusion of Languages," see if you can locate a section where several paragraphs work together to develop one larger idea. (See part 1b for an example.) Photocopy or write out these paragraphs and then answer these questions.

1. What are the paragraphs about?
2. What is the main idea?
3. What is the support given to develop the main idea?

# Chapter 6 Enumeration and Classification Organization

To **enumerate** means to make a list. Writers who use enumeration organization are simply listing ideas that are related to each other one after the other. This is a fairly common technique in textbooks, articles, and other types of academic writing.

## Explanation and Examples

Enumeration is generally used when a writer wants to make a list of points or present a series of ideas about a topic. For example, a writer wants to discuss three benefits of getting a college degree. Using enumeration organization, she would start by presenting the first benefit and discussing it, then introduce the second benefit and discuss it, and conclude by stating and discussing the third benefit. This structure is illustrated by the following outline.

> Topic: Benefits of Getting a College Degree
> 1. benefit one
> 2. benefit two
> 3. benefit three

In many instances, a writer wants to show that one idea can be broken down into several types, or **classifications.** Classification is a special type of enumeration organization because the different items being classified, when combined, make up a whole idea. For example, a writer discussing the structure of the U.S. government might use a classification to discuss the legislative branch, the executive branch, and the judicial branch. Together, these three branches make up the U.S. government. Using a chart helps to illustrate this organization.

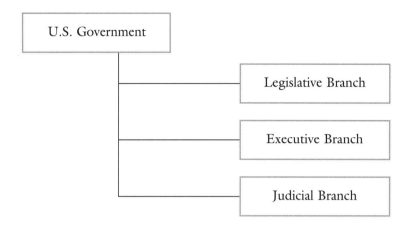

Often there are markers that indicate to the reader that the writer is using an enumeration or classification organization. The most common markers are cardinal numbers (1, 2, 3) and ordinal numbers (*first, second, third*). Other markers might include nouns (*category, class, kind, type*) or verbs (*to categorize, to classify, to divide*).

As is the case for all of the different types of organization examined in this book, sometimes the writer does not use specific markers but only implies this structure, which is most frequently done by the use of parallel structures in a list. For example, look at the following sentence.

> The U.S. government is made up of the <u>legislative branch</u>, the <u>executive branch</u>, and the <u>judicial branch</u>. The judicial branch . . .

Although there is no specific marker to indicate that this text will be organized using a classification structure, the structure of the sentence suggests that the U.S. government is going to be classified into three categories.

**Activity →** The following paragraphs use classification or another type of enumeration as their main organizational structure. For each, identify the main idea that is being broken down into categories. Indicate what type of marker is used to indicate the structure, if any. Then draw a diagram or provide an outline that shows the organizational structure clearly.

*EXAMPLE*

The process of introducing an idea or object that is new to culture is known as ***innovation.*** There are two forms of innovation: discovery and invention. A ***discovery*** involves making known or sharing the existence of an aspect of reality. The finding of the DNA molecule and the identification of a new moon of Saturn are both acts of discovery. . . . By contrast, an ***invention*** results when existing cultural items are combined into a form that did not exist before. The bow and arrow, the automobile, and the television are all examples of inventions. (Schaefer 2000, 50)

Main idea:  <u>Types of innovation</u>

Organizational markers:  <u>"There are two forms of innovation: . . . " "By contrast . . ."</u>

Diagram:

Types of innovation ─────────

> A *discovery* involves making known or sharing the existence of an aspect of reality.

> An *invention* results when existing cultural items are combined into a form.

1. Racial and ethnic groups can relate to one another in a wide variety of ways, ranging from friendships and intermarriage to genocide, from behaviors that require mutual approval to behaviors imposed by a dominant group.

   One devastating pattern of intergroup relations is *genocide*—the deliberate, systematic killing of an entire people or nation. . . .

   The *expulsion* of a people is another extreme means of acting out racial or ethnic prejudice. . . .

   Genocide and expulsion are extreme behaviors. More typical intergroup relations as they occur in North America and throughout the world follow four identifiable patterns: (1) amalgamation, (2) assimilation, (3) segregation, and (4) pluralism. Each pattern defines the dominant group's actions and the minority group's responses. (Schaefer 2000, 233–34)

   Main idea: _____

   Organizational markers: _____

   Diagram or outline:

2. One way to describe [population] movement is by the term **mobility,** the *ability* to move, from one place to another, either permanently or temporarily. Mobility may be used to describe a wide array of human movement ranging from a journey to work . . . to an ocean-spanning, permanent move.

   The second way to describe population movement is in terms of **migration,** a long-distance move to a new location. Migration involves a permanent or temporary change of residence from one neighborhood or settlement . . . to another. Moving from a particular location is defined as **emigration;** this process is also known as *out-migration*. Moving to a particular location is defined as **immigration** or, alternatively, as *in-migration*. (Knox and Marston 1998, 127)

Main idea: _____

Organizational markers: _____

Diagram or outline:

3. You choose to eat many foods simply because you like them. What causes you to like some foods more than others? Your emotions are one factor. You are likely to prefer foods that you associate with positive emotions, such as comfort and caring. However, you are apt to dislike foods that you associate with negative feelings, such as guilt and fear.

   Your genes are partly responsible for your food preferences. You were born with personal preferences for certain tastes and smells. Everyone has taste buds that sense the tastes of sweet, salty, sour, and bitter. Just how you perceive each of these tastes, however, is part of your unique makeup. For instance, one person might wince in pain from the heat he or she feels when eating a jalapeño pepper. However, another person might hardly seem to notice the heat when eating one of these peppers. This difference in taste perception is due to genetics. It helps explain why members of the same family who have the same background often prefer different foods.

   Although genes play an important role in determining taste preferences, your experiences with food affect your preferences, too. Suppose someone offers you a choice between fried grasshoppers and a hamburger. If you have eaten hamburgers but have never tried grasshoppers, you are more likely to choose the hamburger. Someone from China, where fried grasshoppers are a delicacy, might be more likely to choose the grasshoppers. People simply prefer what is familiar to them. (West 2000, 34–35)

   New idea: _____

   Organizational markers: _____

   Diagram or outline:

4. On the basis of analyses of rocks and fossils, the last billion years have been divided into three *geological eras:* the Paleozoic, the oldest, dating from about 220 million years and older; the middle era, or Mesozoic, from about 220 million to 65 million years ago; and the Cenozoic, which began approximately 65 million years ago and still continues. (de Blij and Murphy 1999, 36)

Main idea: _____

Organizational markers: _____

Diagram or outline:

## Putting It into Practice ▎▎▎

**Part 1.** In the textbook chapter in appendix 1, "Ecosystems: How They Work," locate four examples of information organized with enumeration or classification structure. Photocopy or write out the examples on a separate sheet of paper. Indicate the controlling idea as well as any markers that indicate the organization structure being used. Then draw a diagram that represents the structure of the text.

**Part 2:** Using a textbook that you are reading for an academic class, other materials assigned by your instructor, or the textbook chapter in appendix 2 titled "The Diffusion of Languages," locate at least two examples of text organized with enumeration or classification structure. Photocopy or write out each example. For each, identify the controlling idea as well as any markers that indicate the organization structure being used. Then draw a diagram that represents the structure of the text.

# Chapter 7 COMPARISON-CONTRAST ORGANIZATION

Authors frequently use a comparison-contrast structure when they want to emphasize the similarity or differences—or both—among people, ideas, or things. A comparison focuses on how two or more things are similar, while a contrast emphasizes the differences.

## Explanation and Examples

In the following paragraph, the author defines two different types of cultural diffusion by contrasting them.

> In hierarchical diffusion, ideas leapfrog from one important person to another or from one urban center to another, temporarily bypassing other persons or rural territory. We can see hierarchical diffusion at work in everyday life by observing the acceptance of new modes of dress or hairstyles. **By contrast,** contagious diffusion involves the wavelike spread of ideas, without regard to hierarchies, in the manner of a contagious diseases. (Jordan-Bychkov and Domosh 1999, 15)

In order to understand the main idea in this paragraph it is important to recognize that the author is contrasting two different ways in which ideas spread, or diffuse. Drawing a chart is a good way to represent the contrast that is being made.

Point of Contrast: **How Ideas Spread**

| Hierarchical Diffusion | | Contagious Diffusion |
|---|---|---|
| ideas spread from one important person or areas to another, temporarily bypassing less important people or areas | ←**By contrast**→ | ideas spread from person to person, in a wavelike manner (not bypassing anyone) |

Whenever a comparison-contrast relationship is being expressed, the key to understanding this relationship is to understand what the point of comparison or contrast is. The details of the paragraph then usually support one side or the other of the comparison-contrast.

As the use of *by contrast* in the example paragraph above illustrates, often a word or phrase serves as a marker indicating that a comparison or a contrast is being made. These words are a clue that the author is using a comparison-contrast structure to organize the key ideas. Below is a list of words that are frequently used to indicate comparison and contrast.

---

**Signals of Comparison**

| | | |
|---|---|---|
| like | just like | just as |
| alike | likewise | equally |
| resembles | also | similarly |
| the same | similar | identical |
| parallel | comparable | common |
| equivalent | resemble | in common |
| in the same way | likewise | like |
| as (adjective) as | | |

**Signals of Contrast**

| | | |
|---|---|---|
| however | in contrast | instead |
| on the other hand | as opposed to | unlike |
| different | differently | to differ from |
| to distinguish | distinction | difference |
| to contrast with | to oppose | while |
| whereas | rather than | but |
| yet | conversely | |
| unlike (noun phrase) | | |
| in contrast to (noun phrase) | on the one hand . . . on the other hand | |
| | Not all/every . . . some/many/much/a few | |

---

As you can see from these lists, words that signal comparison or contrast can occur in a variety of grammatical functions. For example, they can be **verbs:** "X *resembles* Y"; they can be **nouns:** "X and Y have many *similarities*"; they can be **adjectives:** "X is *equivalent to* Y"; they can be **adverbs:** "X and Y are *equally* funny"; or they can be **conjunctions** or other types of clause connectors: "X is similar to this; *likewise,* Y is similar to this."

However, the comparison or the contrast may not be explicitly indicated by one of these signal words; it may only be implied by the relationship of the information in the text. Look at the following example.

In order to understand the expansion patterns of Islam, Christianity and Judaism—the three great monotheistic faiths—it is helpful to look first at their views on proselytizing. Christians and Muslims have historically viewed conversion to their faiths, whether by persuasion or force, as a key objective. As Judaism has remained primarily an ethnic religion throughout its history, they do not actively seek new converts. In fact, it is quite difficult to become a Jew by conversion.

In this paragraph, there is no explicit signal that indicates a comparison or contrast is being made. However, by reading carefully, you can see that there is a point of comparison and contrast (views on proselytizing), with Christianity being compared with Islam and both of these religions contrasted with Judaism. The following chart shows the comparison and contrast that is being made.

Point of Comparison-Contrast: **Views on Proselytizing**

| Islam | | Christianity |
|---|---|---|
| Conversion by persuasion or force has historically been a key objective. | ←compared with→ | Conversion by persuasion or force has historically been a key objective. |

contrasted with

| Judaism |
|---|
| Does not actively seek new converts. |

**Activity →** **Part 1.** In each of the sentences below, circle the word or words that signal a comparison or contrast. Underline the specific detail given to show the similarities or differences between the two points. Then complete the sentence that follows, indicating what two ideas are being compared or contrasted and what the point of comparison-contrast is.

*EXAMPLE*

**Ascribed status** is a social position "assigned" to a person without regard for that person's unique characteristics or talents. (By contrast,) **achieved status** is a social position attained by a person largely through his or her own effort. (Schaefer 2000, 185)

> NOTE: Ascribed status is being (compared to/ (contrasted with)) achieved status based on how the status is attained.

1. In general terms, migrants make their decisions to move based on push factors and pull factors. Push factors are events and conditions that impel an individual to move *from* a location. They include a wide variety of possible motives, from the idiosyncratic, such as an individual migrant's dissatisfaction with the amenities offered at home, to the dramatic, such as war, economic dislocation, or ecological deterioration. Pull factors are forces of attraction that influence migrants to move *to* a particular location. Factors drawing individual migrants to chosen destinations, again, may range from the highly personal (such as a strong desire to live near the sea) to the very structural (such as strong

economic growth, and thus relatively lucrative job opportunities). (Knox and
Marston 1998, 127)

_____ is being (compared to/contrasted with)

_____ based on _____ .

2. The very first computers did not have the ability to save information. When
you unplugged them, all of the data vanished. The early computers used holes
punched in cards to represent data. Computer users were often seen carrying
their programming cards around in shoe boxes. Today, "floppy" and "hard"
disks are used. Removable cartridges, also common, are hard disks enclosed in
a plastic shell. They may be removed from the drive and transported like floppy
disks. Optical disks have become a very good means of storing large amounts
of data. These include compact audio disks (CDs) and CD-ROMs. . . .

At the same time, the memory inside the computer has increased dramatically.
Today, a desktop computer may have more than 1000 times as much memory as
did the first desktop computers in the 1970s. This means computer programs
can be much, much larger. Today's desktop computers are far more powerful
than those that occupied several large rooms several decades ago! (Sanders
1997, 38–39)

_____ is being (compared to/contrasted with)

_____ based on _____ .

3. About 10,000 years ago, in certain parts of the world, basic changes occurred in
the way people lived. The period that began then is called the New Stone Age,
or Neolithic Age. Its scientific name comes from the Greek words *neos,* meaning
"new," and *lithos,* meaning "stone."

In the Old Stone Age and Middle Stone Age, people chipped stone to
produce an edge or a point. In the New Stone Age, people discovered a better
way to make tools and weapons. They learned how to use a flat piece of
sandstone to polish stones to a fine edge or a sharp point. They learned to make
tools from wood and from many kinds of stone. With these new methods and
materials, they could make special tools—awls, wedges, saws, drills, chisels, and
needles.

But other far more important changes occurred during the New Stone Age.
Earlier people had been **nomads,** or wanderers who travel from place to place in
search of food. Neolithic people, however, began settling in permanent villages
because of two important developments: (1) the taming of several additional
kinds of animals, and (2) the development of agriculture. (Mazour and Peoples
1990, 8)

_____ are being (compared to/contrasted with)

_____ based on _____ .

4. Different territorial characteristics can present opportunities and challenges, depending on the historical and political-economic context. Thus, the United States' large size, large population, and abundant resources helped it emerge as a major global power. For the former Soviet Union, however, the vast distances over which people and resources were distributed presented a serious obstacle and helped bring about its collapse. Similar contrasts can be seen when the issue of shape is considered. Particularly before the advent of modern transportation and communication, it was easier for a central government to knit together the territory of a *compact* state—one in which the distance from the geometric center to any point on the boundary did not vary greatly—than it was for states lacking this characteristic. Some states are *fragmented*, consisting of two or more separate pieces; examples include the Philippines and East and West Pakistan before they were divided. This fragmentation makes certain kinds of interactions more difficult. Other states are *elongated* or attenuated (Chile, Vietnam), with historical consequences that are still evident today. Still others have a *protruted* area—one that extends out from a more compact core; this area sometimes has developed in different ways from the core (e.g., the southern portion of Thailand). Such states are sometimes called *prorupt states.* Finally, a few states are *perforated* by another country (e.g., South Africa by Lesotho, Italy by San Marino and Vatican City). (de Blij and Murphy 1999, 346–47)

A. _____ is being (compared to/contrasted with)

_____ based on _____ .

B. _____ , _____ , _____ , _____ ,

_____ , and _____ are being (compared/contrasted)

based on _____ .

**Part 2.** In both of the following paragraphs, a contrast is being made that is not explicitly indicated by signal words. After each paragraph, indicate what two ideas are being contrasted and what the point of contrast is.

1. India's blast shook the world out of its post-cold-war complacency. The nuclear standoff between the Americans and the Russians was scary, but it was also stable. The nuclear club was limited to five members: the United States, Soviet Union, China, France, and Britain. Other nations found it prudent to stand under the nuclear umbrella of a superpower, rather than develop their own weapons. India could be a harbinger of a more chaotic world order, of rivalrous nationalities scrambling to arm themselves with the bomb. Think of Europe in August 1914, only with weapons of mass destruction. (Thomas 1998, 30)

_____ is being (compared to/contrasted with)

_____ based on _____ .

2. A *claim* is something that is stated as fact. In the example the manufacturer claimed that the watch would run even after coming in contact with water. When you *warrant,* or guarantee, your claim, you are letting the person know that what you claim is believable. Thus, when you make a *warranted claim,* you are stating something as fact that has a basis in truth and can be proven.

An *unwarranted claim* is a statement that does not have any facts to support it. This does not mean that all unwarranted claims are false. But even if a claim is true, it must be considered unwarranted if no evidence is presented to back it up. For example, if you buy a watch that claims to be waterproof but does not come with warranty, you will be taking a risk. The watch may be waterproof, but you have nothing to back up that claim. (Farah and Karls 1990, 185)

_____ is being (compared to/contrasted with)

_____ based on _____ .

## Putting It into Practice ▌▐ ▌

**Part 1.** In the textbook chapter in appendix 1, "Ecosystems: How They Work," locate two passages in which the text is structured by comparison or contrast. Photocopy or write out the examples on a separate sheet of paper. Circle the words that signal that a comparison or contrast is being made. Underline the specific detail given that shows the similarities or differences between the two points. Then write a summary sentence (like those after each paragraph in the activity section above) indicating what two ideas are being compared or contrasted and what the point of comparison or contrast is.

**Part 2.** Using a textbook that you are reading for an academic class, other materials assigned by your instructor, or the textbook chapter in appendix 2 titled "The Diffusion of Languages," locate at least three examples of paragraphs that use a comparison-contrast structure. Photocopy, type, or write out each paragraph. For each paragraph, circle the word or words that signal a comparison or contrast. Underline the specific detail given that shows the similarities or differences between the two things being compared or contrasted. Then write a summary sentence (like those after each paragraph in the activity section above) indicating what two ideas are being compared/contrasted and what the point of comparison or contrast is.

# Chapter 8 Time Order and Cause-and-Effect Organization

Ideas can be related to each other by when they occur in time. Time relationships can be expressed in two ways. **Time order** is used to indicate how ideas or events occur in relationship to others; for example, did one event happen before another in time? **Cause-and-effect relationships** are used to describe how one event, occurring first, led to or caused another later event. Both of these types of organization are frequently used in academic textbooks, especially in the sciences.

## Explanation and Examples

1. **Time Order Organization:** When we put events in time order, we are arranging them by when they occurred or will occur. Many of the words that signal that a time order organization is being used have already been introduced in chapter 4. Flip back to table 4.1 and review the various logical connectors, and their grammatical roles, that express a time relationship between ideas. Other typical signals for this type of organization include specific dates and times and words such as *steps, process, series,* and *stages.* In example 1a below, words like *earliest, then, in turn,* and *eventually* mark the time sequence.

   Time order organization can be used in two ways. The first is to *present a series of events in the order in which they occurred.* This time order is important and must be recognized in order to understand the main ideas. The following paragraph provides an example, with the word clues showing the time organization underlined.

   1a. The <u>earliest</u> known alphabet was the North Semitic alphabet, which developed around 1700 B.C. in Palestine and Syria. It consisted of 22 consonantal letters. The Hebrew, Arabic, and Phoenician alphabets <u>were based</u> on this model. <u>Then</u> around 1000 B.C., the Greeks added vowels to the Phoenician alphabet. The Greek alphabet <u>in turn</u> became the model for the Etruscan alphabet used in parts of what is now Italy (ca. 800 B.C.), and the Etruscan alphabet <u>eventually</u> provided the letters for the ancient Roman alphabet. (Bergman 1995, 242.)

The main idea of this paragraph is how the Roman alphabet (which the English alphabet is based on) evolved from the earliest known alphabet. We can also see that five events in time are described, in this order.

1. The <u>earliest</u> alphabet was the North Semitic alphabet.
2. The Phoenician alphabet <u>was based</u> on this alphabet.
3. The Greeks <u>then</u> added vowels to make their alphabet.
4. <u>In turn</u>, the Etruscan alphabet used the Greek alphabet as a model.
5. <u>Eventually</u>, the Roman alphabet evolved from the Etruscan alphabet.

The second way that the time order organizational pattern can be used is to show the steps in a process. Usually, the order of details is very important when describing a process, and so is typically well marked by signal words. The following paragraph provides an example, with the word clues showing the sequential organization underlined:

1b.  Bones are produced from cartilage. During embryonic development, the human skeleton <u>first</u> appears almost as a cartilage "scale model." <u>Gradually,</u> this cartilage "model" <u>is replaced by</u> bone. (Miller and Levine 1998b, 49)

The main idea of this paragraph is the process by which bones are made, which occurs in these two steps:

1. <u>First</u>, in the embryo the skeleton appears as cartilage.
2. <u>Gradually</u>, the cartilage <u>is replaced by</u> bone.

2. **Cause-and-Effect Organization:** Cause-and-effect organization also expresses a time relationship between two actions or events with one additional important feature: one event **causes** another event to occur. As with time order organization, many of the words that signal cause and effect were introduced in table 4.1 in chapter 4. Go back and review them.

   Typically, this organizational pattern focuses on either the causes for some event or the effects that are a direct result of it. The following is an example of a paragraph that focuses on effects: how the dermis—a layer of our skin—reacts to changes in temperature.

2a.  The dermis reacts to the body's needs in a number of ways. For example, on cold days—when you need to conserve heat—blood vessels in the dermis narrow, limiting the loss of heat. When the body is hot, the same vessels widen, bringing more blood to the skin. This warms the skin, causing the loss of heat. (Miller and Levine 1998b, 46)

The examples in this paragraph show how temperature changes affect the dermis. These effects include

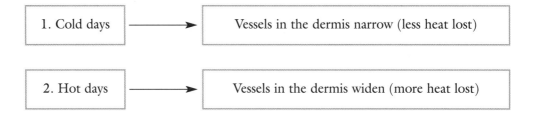

The next paragraph focuses on the causes for the development of strong fears.

2b. What accounts for such strong fears? One possibility involves the process of *classical conditioning. . . .* Through such learning, stimuli that could not initially elicit strong emotional reactions can often come to do so. For example, a person may acquire an intense fear of bees or wasps after seeing a friend or relative stung by such an insect. (Rings and Kremer 2000, 627)

The main idea of this paragraph is how people can develop strong fears through a process called "classical conditioning." The example illustrates how this can happen.

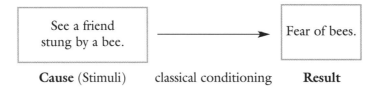

3. **Complex Organization:** You should be aware that writers may use more than one organizational structure at a time to present their ideas. Notice how the writer of the paragraph in example 3a *combines* both a cause-and-effect structure and a time order structure to present ideas.

3a. When death actually occurs, the response to it may take place in several phases. Four successive phases of emotions that typically accompany loss have been identified: first, shock, a kind of numbed refusal to acknowledge that anything has happened; second, protest, often accompanied by anticipating the dead person's reappearance; third, despair, frequently in the form of severe depression; and finally, adaptation, in which the survivor attempts to build a new life. (Popenoe 2000, 135)

In this paragraph, the main focus is on the response (result) people have to the death of a loved one. This response, however, occurs in four stages. The structure of this paragraph can be illustrated as follows.

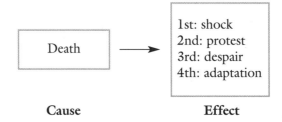

**Activity →**

- For each of the following, determine whether the paragraph is using time order or cause-and-effect organization.
- Underline the words that signal the type of organization being used.
- Indicate the main idea and then draw a diagram or write an outline showing how the main idea and details are related.

For time order, be sure to indicate whether the passage is describing a series of events in time or steps in a process.

For cause and effect, be sure to indicate whether the focus is on causes or effects.

If other organizational structures are also being used, be sure to indicate this fact as well.

The passage below was used in chapter 7 as an example of how two factors for migration, push and pull, can be contrasted. If you read the paragraph again, you will see that this paragraph also is structured using cause and effect.

*EXAMPLE*

In general terms, migrants make their decisions to move based on push factors and pull factors. **Push factors** are <u>events and conditions that impel</u> an individual to move *from* a location. They include a wide variety of <u>possible motives</u>, from the idiosyncratic, such as an individual migrant's dissatisfaction with the amenities offered at home, to the dramatic, such as war, economic dislocation, or ecological deterioration. **Pull factors** are <u>forces of attraction that influence</u> migrants to move *to* a particular location. <u>Factors drawing</u> individual migrants to chosen destinations, again, may range from the highly personal (such as a strong desire to live near the sea) to the very structural (such as strong economic growth, and thus relatively lucrative job opportunities). (Knox and Marston 1998, 127)

Organizational pattern: <u>*Cause and effect (and contrast)*</u>

Main idea: <u>*The effect of "push" factors and the effect of "pull" factors*</u>

<u>*on migration*</u>

Diagram or outline of ideas:

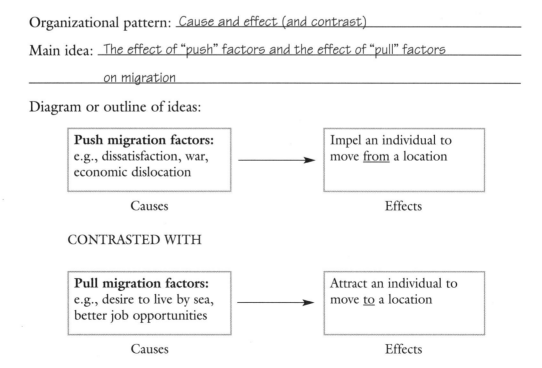

1. The link between stress and personal health, according to medical experts, is very strong (Kiecolt & Glaser, 1992). Some authorities estimate that stress plays some role in 50 to 70 percent of all physical illness (Frese, 1985). Moreover, included in these percentages are some of the most serious and life-threatening ailments known to medical science. To list just a few, stress has been implicated in the occurrence of heart disease, hardening of the arteries, and even diabetes. (Rings and Kremer 2000, 580)

Organizational pattern: _____

Main idea: _____

Diagram or outline of ideas:

2. Various birds evolved ways in which to run and swim. However, unlike almost all other vertebrates, most birds can fly. Birds can fly because of their relatively light bodies, powerful breast muscles, and aerodynamic feathers and wings.

    First, birds are lighter than other vertebrates mainly because of their bones, which have spaces within them. In addition, air sacs used in breathing extend inside several bones, making these bones even lighter. Birds minimize their body mass in other ways, too. Sex organs, for example, are small and light most of the year, then increase to working size during breeding season.

    Second, birds have large, strong breast muscles, which they use to flap their wings. These huge muscles provide the force that lifts a bird into the air.

    Third, a bird's wings and feathers are shaped in just the right way for flight. (Miller and Levine 1998a, 93)

Organizational pattern: _____

Main idea: _____

Diagram or outline of ideas:

3. At the stratified site of Ali Kosh, what is now southwestern Iran, we see the remains of a community that started out about 7500 B.C. living mostly on wild plants and animals. Over the next two thousand years, until about 5500 B.C., agriculture and herding became increasingly important. After 5500 B.C. we see the appearance of two innovations—irrigation and the use of domesticated cattle—that seem to have stimulated a minor population explosion during the following millennium. (Ember and Ember 2000, 121)

Organizational pattern: _____

Main idea: _____

Diagram or outline of ideas:

4. Increasing the average wealth of a population affects the environment both positively and negatively. An affluent country certainly can and does provide such things as safe drinking water, sanitary sewage systems and sewage treatment, and collection and disposal of refuse. Thus, in terms of the most immediate forms of human wastes, pollution decreases, and the environment we live in improves with increasing affluence. In addition, if we can afford gas and electricity, we are not destroying our parks and woodlands for firewood. In short, we are able to afford conservation and management, better agricultural practices, and so on, that in many respects improve our environment.

   But affluence does have its negative aspects as well. For example, by using large quantities of fossil fuel (coal, oil, and natural gas) to drive our cars, heat and cool our homes, generate electricity, and so on, the United States is responsible for a large share of the production of carbon dioxide. (Nebel and Wright 1998, 152–53)

Organizational pattern: _____

Main idea: _____

Diagram or outline of ideas:

5. Whenever you can assume that your audience will be interested in what you have to say, or at least willing to cooperate with you, your message should follow the direct, or deductive, plan. You should present the request or the main idea first, follow up with necessary details, and close with a cordial statement of the action you want. This approach works well when your request requires no special tact or persuasion. (Thill and Bovée 1993, 123)

Organizational pattern: _____

Main idea: _____

Diagram or outline of ideas:

6. Without a computer, we can picture the simulation as follows: First, the numbers from 1 to 1,000 are written on 1,000 slips of paper. . . . Then, a random sample of size $n = 15$ is drawn without replacement from this population and its values are recorded. We replace the sample before the next one is drawn, and we repeat this process until 100 random samples have been obtained. (Freund 2001, 278)

Organizational pattern: _____

Main idea: _____

Diagram or outline of ideas:

## Putting It into Practice ▌▌▌

**Part 1a.** The textbook chapter in appendix 1, "Ecosystems: How They Work," describes several processes that have a time order structure. The carbon cycle (p. 66), the phosphorus cycle (pp. 66–68), and the nitrogen cycle (pp. 68–70) are all fairly complex processes that are illustrated in figures 3-14, 3-15, and 3-16 (pp. 67–69). Photocopy, type, or write out on a separate sheet of paper the first paragraph in the section describing the carbon cycle on page 66 and the second paragraph in the section describing the phosphorus cycle, which is on page 67. Circle all the words that indicate a time order sequence. Draw a diagram or provide an outline that represents the processes described in these paragraphs (which is much simpler than what is shown in figures 3-14 and 3-15, pp. 67–68).

**Part 1b.** The textbook chapter in appendix 1, "Ecosystems: How They Work," gives many examples of ideas ordered in a cause-and-effect structure. Locate at least two sections of text organized around a cause-and-effect structure. Photocopy, type, or write out the examples on a separate sheet of paper. Circle the words that signal the organizational structure. Draw a diagram that represents the organizational structure.

**Part 2.** Using a textbook that you are reading for an academic class, other materials assigned by your instructor, or the textbook chapter in appendix 2 titled "The Diffusion of Languages," locate *at least one paragraph* that uses time order structure **and** *at least one paragraph* that uses cause-and-effect structure. Photocopy, type, or write out each paragraph. Circle the words that signal the organizational structure and then draw a diagram that represents the organizational structure.

# Part 3
## READING TO STUDY

As a student, you need to be able to do more than read a textbook and have a general understanding of its main idea; you often have to understand and remember a lot of very challenging information. This is not an easy task, but the ability to accomplish it is the difference between doing well in school and doing poorly. The chapters in this part focus on things you can do to help you *study* textbooks, not just read them.

To be a better reader, you must learn to be aware of what you are doing when you are reading and look for ways to read more effectively. Chapter 9 looks at strategies that successful readers use to help them to read quickly with good understanding; this chapter also gives you practice in applying these strategies to your own reading.

Chapter 10 introduces a popular study technique designed to help you fully understand the texts you read so that you are better prepared for tests.

Chapter 11 goes one step further and introduces a technique that will help you improve your note-taking skills.

# Chapter 9 IMPROVING STUDY SKILLS: INTRODUCTION TO READING STRATEGIES

Research has shown that within twenty minutes the average student forgets about 50 percent of all **new** class information he or she has read or heard, and that within six days 75 percent is forgotten. This is certainly discouraging to think about, especially when you have just spent the last two hours reading a chapter for one of your classes. Two of the reasons that students forget so much are (1) they are **not prepared** to study what they have read, and (2) they **do not have a plan** to help them learn and remember the information they are reading. Studying is much more than just following the words on a page!

According to the research, what do successful academic readers do?

1. Successful academic readers are **active** readers. They don't just passively read words. They *ask questions* about what they read, they *take notes*, they try to *connect* what they are reading to what they already know, and they *check* to make sure they understood what they have read.

2. Successful academic readers are **strategic** readers. They read a text for a specific purpose (e.g., to prepare for a test) with specific goals in mind (e.g., to understand the main ideas). They use *prereading* strategies to prepare them for the reading (e.g., skim the text to make predictions and determine structure), they use *during-reading* strategies to help them understand what has been written (e.g., look for main ideas), and they use *after-reading* strategies to help them remember (e.g., review notes).

3. Successful academic readers are **metacognitive** readers. Metacognition is your awareness of your own learning and thinking. Metacognitive readers

   a. *monitor* how well they understand what they read ("Does this make sense?")

   b. *recognize* when they do not understand something ("I don't get this.")

c. *look for* ways to help them understand what they are having trouble with ("I'm going to read this again more slowly.").

In chapter 10 we will introduce a study technique that will help you to be more active and strategic as you read academic texts. In this chapter we will look at ways to develop your metacognitive strategies as you read, as well as introduce general reading strategies used by successful academic readers.

## Explanation and Examples

A metacognitive reader knows not only *what* types of reading strategies will work, but also *when* and *where* to use them. The goal of this chapter is to help you recognize and use metacognitive strategies that will best increase your learning and test scores.

Metacognition—your awareness of what you are learning and thinking—can be divided into four types: **self-awareness, task awareness, comprehension awareness,** and **strategy awareness.**

1. **Self-Awareness:** Being self-aware is knowing your strengths and weaknesses as a reader, and making efforts to figure out what will make you a more successful student. No two readers have exactly the same strengths and weaknesses; and no two people learn in exactly the same way. When you are metacognitively self-aware, you observe what you do as you read and learn, and then reflect on what works for you, what does not, and why.

**Activity → 1**

Answer the following questions, and then discuss them with your classmates:

1. Do you find it difficult to get started on reading assignments? Do you frequently put off work you should do? If so, why? What can you do to change this?

2. Do you find one subject (e.g., science, history) harder to read than another? If so, why?

3. Do you have trouble staying awake when you study? If so, why? What can you do to change this?

4. Do you find that when you read, your mind wanders and you start thinking about other things? If so, why? What can you do to change this?

5. Do other people or activities distract you when you read? If so, why? What can you do to change this?

Don't be discouraged if you find that you do have trouble concentrating and staying focused. The trick is finding the right place and time to read, getting rid of distractions, and learning to focus your concentration as you read. All readers lose their concentration from time to time, but as you become more aware of when and why you lose focus, you will improve your ability to refocus your attention.

2. **Task-Awareness:** Task awareness is having a clear understanding of the task that you are required to do. This includes knowing how long it will take you, how difficult it will be, what exactly it is you are supposed to accomplish, and what it will take to accomplish it successfully. Knowing what you are supposed to do for an assignment is very important because it helps you determine how carefully to read and how much time to give to it. For example, you can probably read a textbook chapter more quickly if you need to prepare for a class discussion than if you are preparing for an exam on the material.

**Activity → 2**

Most likely, your instructor asked you to read this chapter before class. Stop for a minute and respond to the following questions about the assignment your instructor gave you and jot down your answers on a separate sheet of paper. In class, discuss your answers with your classmates to see how they answered these questions.

1. How long is the reading assignment? How many pages do you have to read?
2. What exactly is it that you are supposed to do? Restate the assignment in your own words.
3. What steps will you go through to accomplish the task? List them.
4. How are you going to be evaluated? What will the instructor do to see if you have accomplished the task or have learned the material?
5. How long do you think it will take you to do this assignment? Keep track of the time and see if you were right.
6. How difficult do you think the task will be? Why do you think so?

3. **Comprehension Awareness:** Comprehension awareness is simply monitoring your own understanding of what you are reading, recognizing when you don't understand something, and then trying to do something about it. When you read, if you say to yourself things like, "Let me see if I understand this point," or "I don't get this," or "I'm going to read this again more slowly," then you are aware of your comprehension process. Once you recognize you are having trouble understanding something, then you need to be aware of strategies that help you improve your comprehension. These are discussed next.

4. **Strategy Awareness:** Strategy awareness is knowing *what* reading and study strategies you can and should use—as well as *when* and *where* to use them—in order to complete successfully an assignment. In a sense, everything in this book is designed to teach you strategies you can use to be a more successful reader. In addition, table 9.1 has a list of reading strategies that many successful readers use. The trick is to recognize which strategies will be most useful to accomplish your task . . . and then use them!

**TABLE 9.1.  Reading Strategies for Successful Readers**

**Prereading**

1. Plan a goal for each reading (What do you want to get out of the text?)
2. Overview the text (skim)

   A. Note characteristics of the text, such as length and structure
   B. Note important headings/parts (What information will be covered?)
   C. Note information that is important to your reading goal

3. Decide *what* to read and in *what order*

   A. *Only* sections likely to be important to your goals OR
   B. Certain sections *before* others (such as the abstract, introduction, and conclusion of a scientific article)

4. Mentally note what you learned from the prereading
5. Consider what you already know about the topic (activate your prior knowledge)

**While Reading**

*Use a combination of reading styles*

1. Read the text straight through, from beginning to end

   A. Keep a steady pace OR
   B. If the text is easy, increase your reading speed UNTIL something goes wrong (For example, you miss or do not understand important meanings)

2. Skim the text from beginning to end at a faster pace than number 1 above

   A. Read only for main ideas
   B. Read more slowly for important/difficult information

3. Scan the text, reading only selected sections based on your prior knowledge and prereading decisions

*Use a combination of skills and strategies*

1. Read aloud
2. Look for patterns that the author uses to help you understand (ways of defining, lists of examples, idea/paragraph development, etc.)
3. Repeat/restate difficult ideas immediately after reading them

   A. To remember the ideas better
   B. To complete your understanding of the ideas

4. Paraphrase sections

   a. To understand the overall structure
   b. To use related words, concepts, or ideas in your own sentences

5. Pause to think about the text

*Use the text and main ideas to help your understanding*

1. As you begin to read

   A. Ask, "What is the overall paragraph/text meaning?"
   B. Ask, "Do I understand the paragraph/text's structure?"
   C. Based on your answers, predict how the content and structure will develop

**TABLE 9.1—***Continued*

2. Adjust your answers as you read more of the text

   A. Are previous answers still accurate based on new information?
   B. What specific new information supports or does not support your answers?
   C. Do structural clues support the adjusted answers?
      (For example, is the author's summary or conclusion consistent with your new understanding of the text?)

3. What is your final understanding of the text based on content and structure? (Remember to include information you did *not* expect to find)

*Identify Important Information*

1. Use terms you already know in a text to build your understanding of important new ideas
2. Look for and learn the key words of a text
3. Look for topic sentences
4. Look for topic paragraphs
5. Copy key sentences
6. Highlight, underline, circle, make notes, or outline important points, including important examples
7. Note references in the text that should be looked at or considered later

*Make Conscious Inferences*

1. Know the referent of a pronoun
2. Infer the meanings of new words by using internal (root words, prefixes, etc.) and external (neighboring words, main idea, etc.) clues
3. Infer global meanings of a text's words and sentences, not just their literal meanings
4. Relate information in the text to your prior knowledge

   A. Explain the text using your prior knowledge
   B. Create your own examples of concepts in the text
   C. Broaden specific ideas in the text based on your prior knowledge
   D. Relate events, objects, setting, words, phrases, etc. in the new text to previous texts you have read
   E. Relate this text's content to important themes in a field/profession
   F. Relate this text's content to personally important prior knowledge
      (For example, your own theories, writings, experiences)

5. Make inferences about the author

   A. What are this author's assumptions, worldviews, beliefs, motives?
   B. What is her/his personal background? Professional reputation?
   C. What are her/his strategies in constructing the text?
   D. What is this author's expertise in this content area?

*Integrate Different Parts of the Text*

1. Try to understand the "big picture" of the text's meaning before you try to understand how the details are organized
2. Recognize the main idea of the text and the components that support it

   A. Do the main points work together to support the overall meaning?
   B. Is there cohesion from one sentence/paragraph/section to the next?
   C. Does each sentence/paragraph/section develop logically?

*(continued)*

**TABLE 9.1—*Continued***

3. Use your knowledge of texts

   A. Note the text's overall structure (cause/effect, compare/contrast, etc.)
   B. Note the different parts of the text (introduction, examples, transitions, etc.) and how they interrelate (Is this still part of the introduction, or is this the first topic? This sounds like a summary—is it the conclusion?)
   C. Use the methods of text development to help your comprehension across paragraphs (This paragraph is listing similarities. Will the next paragraph list the differences?)
   D. Note paragraph elements that support a difficult paragraph (Examples, categories, extended definitions, etc.)
   E. Use logical connectors to clarify content and text organization ("First of all," "On the other hand," "In conclusion")

4. Use other parts of the text to help you understand difficult passages

   A. Use tables, figures, footnotes
   B. Jump forward to look for information that will help your understanding of what you have already read
   C. Jump backward to review/understand information that is important to the remaining text
   D. Go back and forth in the text to notice similarities, differences, and logical progressions between the various sections

5. Make a visual aid to help you recognize integrations

   A. Create an outline
   B. Draw a diagram

**Postreading**

1. Read the text again

   A. Closely OR
   B. Scanning for particular information OR
   C. Skimming to confirm your comprehension of the overall meaning

2. Paraphrase the text to increase your memory/comprehension of it
3. List pieces of information found in the text
4. Construct a cohesive summary of the text
5. Ask yourself questions over the content
6. Create your own examples, scenarios, etc. based on the text's information
7. Continue to evaluate and possibly reconstruct your understanding of the text

*Source:* Adapted from Michael Pressley and Peter Afflerbach, *Verbal Protocols of Reading: The Nature of Constructively Responsive Reading* (Hilldale, N.J.: Lawrence Erlbaum Associates, 1995).

**Activity ➔
3**

After looking at table 9.1, answer the following questions and then discuss them with your classmates.

1. What can you do to help you prepare to read (prereading strategies)?

2. What can you do to help you better understand while you read (during-reading strategies)? And what can you do when you are *really* having trouble understanding what you read?

3. What can you do when you are reading and you come across a word you don't know?

4. What can you do to help you better understand what you've read and remember it after you are finished (after-reading strategies)?

5. What can you do if your mind starts to wander and you lose focus while you read?

6. What two strategies listed in table 9.1 have you not used before that might help you? Why do you think so?

## Putting It into Practice ▎▎▎

In chapter 11, you will be taking notes on the textbook chapter in Appendix 1, "Ecosystems: How They Work." While you have read parts of that chapter already, your task now is to read the chapter in Appendix 1 all the way through. As part of this assignment, answer the following questions about your metacognitive awareness and your general reading strategies. You should read through the questions below *before* you begin your assignment. Some of the questions you will answer before you begin reading your assignment; others you will answer while you are reading or after you finish. Also, look again at table 9.1 and choose two new reading strategies that you haven't used much before and try them as you read this assignment.

Course Title:
Textbook and Chapter Title:

*Self-Awareness*

1. What mental, physical, or emotional distractions do you need to be aware of and address to help you focus better while you read?
2. Where are you studying? Is this the best place to study? Why or why not?
3. When are you studying? Is this the best time of day for you to study? Why or why not?
4. Does your mind sometimes wander while you read? Why?

*Task Awareness*

5. What exactly is the assignment that you have to do? Describe it in your own words.
6. How long do you think it will take you to complete it? Time yourself to see whether your prediction was accurate.
7. How difficult do you think this reading assignment is, based on the length, vocabulary, subject matter, and your interest in the topic? (easy, average, or difficult)
8. Having finished, how well do you think you accomplished the assignment? Why?

*Comprehension Awareness*

9. Having finished the assignment, how well do you think you understood what you read?
10. Were there any specific parts of the reading assignment you had trouble understanding? Indicate where and why you had trouble.
11. Were there any words you didn't know? Indicate which ones.

*Strategy Awareness*

12. What do you do to help you stay focused while you read? Does it help?
13. What do you do when you come across vocabulary you don't know? Does it help?
14. If there is a section that you find difficult to understand, what do you do to help you figure out what the text is saying?
15. Are there any other reading strategies that you can use to better understand the text you are reading? (See table 9.1 for some ideas.)
16. What two new reading strategies did you try to use as you read this assignment? Did they help you? Why or why not?

# Chapter 10 STUDY-READING STRATEGIES: SQ3R

Chapter 9 introduced the importance of learning and using a variety of reading strategies to help you better understand and remember the academic material you read. The chapter emphasized the importance of being an *active, strategic,* and *metacognitive* reader, not someone who passively reads the words on a page. Table 9.1 presented a wide variety of strategies that successful readers typically use.

This chapter introduces a reading and studying technique that is taught in many books and programs. This technique, called **SQ3R,**[1] was developed to help students combine a variety of reading and study strategies in a way that promotes active learning and recall of information.

## Explanation and Examples

Each letter in *SQ3R* relates to one of five steps, which together integrate reading and study techniques that are designed to increase recall:

**S** = Survey, **Q** = Question, **R** = Read, **R** = Recite, and **R** = Review

The five basic steps of the SQ3R technique are described in what follows.

**S—Survey:** Try to become familiar with the organization and general content of the material you are going to read.

- Read the title.
- Read the introduction.
- Read each boldface heading and subheading and the first sentence following each.

---

1. Adapted from F. P. Robinson, "Development of SQ3R Method," in *Effective Study,* 4th ed. (New York: Harper & Row, 1970), pp. 31–36.

- Look at all the maps, charts, figures, and graphs, including their titles and descriptions.
- See if you can figure out how the author has organized the material.
- Read the last paragraph or summary, if there is one.
- Read the end-of-the-chapter questions, if there are any.
- Think about what you already know about this topic and what you would like to find out more about.

After you have surveyed the material, you should know generally what it is about and how it is organized. This prereading activity is quite important because it helps you to know what to expect when you begin reading.

**Q—Question:** Try to form questions that can be answered as you read. The easiest way to do this is to turn each heading into a question. If there are no headings, look for the topic or key idea of the paragraph or section and rephrase it as a question that you will try to answer.

- See if the author has included questions to guide your reading at the beginning of the chapter or included review questions at the end. Use these questions to guide your reading.

- Before you read, develop questions to guide your reading before you read, or use questions that your instructor gave you.

- As you read, write down new questions that come to mind that you will want to answer.

The purpose here is to make sure that you are reading actively and for a purpose, not just moving your eyes across the page. You remember information better when you are trying to clarify a question you ask before you start reading. Such questions also help you to focus your attention. The survey and question steps are the type of *prereading* work done by the successful readers described in table 9.1.

**R—Read:** Read the material section by section.

- As you read, look for the answer to the study questions given by the author or the questions that you developed before you began.

- As new questions come to mind, try to find answers to them as well.

- Look for main ideas and other important information.

- Look for ways to make the material more interesting by thinking about how it applies to your own life.

- Be metacognitive! Think about what you are thinking about as you read: What do you understand? What is confusing? Do you need to read more slowly or carefully? What should you take notes on?

**R—Recite:** After you finish each section (heading, subheading, etc.), stop and reflect on what you've read.

- See if you can answer your questions for the section. Recite the answer to yourself.

- If you can't recite the answer, look back to find it. Then check your recall again.

- Write your answers down in your own words. Take notes on what you are reading. This forces you to think about what you are reading, to look for main ideas, and to summarize important information.

Be sure to complete this step after you read each section. It may seem like a lot of work, but this is the process you have to go through in order to understand and remember what you are reading. With complex material, you may even want to do this step after every paragraph.

**R—Review:** When you have finished the whole reading assignment, review to see what you understood and remembered.

- Go back to each heading or section; look at your questions and try to answer them once again. If you can't recall the answer, look back and find it. Then test yourself again.

- If you are going to be tested on the material you are reading, find time to review your notes as frequently as possible.

Studies have shown that memory and understanding of material increase dramatically if you take a few minutes to review it right after you have read it, rather than wait until later when you are studying for a test. If you wait until later, it's almost like reading it for the first time.

Although this SQ3R technique may sound like a lot of work, once you become familiar and comfortable with it, you will save time, as you will learn and remember information more quickly and efficiently. Once you become efficient at using SQ3R, you will be automatically asking and answering questions about what you are reading. When you combine this SQ3R method with the note-taking method discussed in chapter 11, you should be much more effective in taking notes and studying for exams.

Here is an example of how the SQ3R method can be used. First, look at the textbook chapter in appendix 1, "Ecosystems: How They Work." Then follow the step-by-step example below of how one could use SQ3R to carefully read this text.

## S—Survey

Read the title of the chapter, the "Key Issues and Questions" section, the introduction, each boldface heading, and the review questions at the end of the chapter.

1. What is the chapter about?
   This chapter explains the physical and chemical elements and processes that make ecosystems work.

2. What *major* topics are included?
   The major headings are "Elements, Life, and Energy"; "Principles of Ecosystem Function"; "Implications for Humans."

3. How does this textbook help you with this "survey" process?
   Clear headings and subheadings are given, and important concepts are in bold. Guiding questions and key issues are listed at the beginning of the chapter. There are many diagrams and figures.

## Q—Question

Turn the headings and subheadings for the first couple of sections into questions. Remember the "wh" questions: who, what, when, where, why, and how.

*Questions*

What are elements? How are these related to "life" and "energy"?
What's the difference between living and nonliving systems?
What role does energy play in the ecosystem?

## R—Read

Read the material following the heading and the subheadings, looking for the answers to your questions. Look for key ideas and other important information. Think about how this applies to your own life.

*Key ideas:* matter, atoms, elements, molecules, compounds, minerals, organic and inorganic molecules.

*How this applies to me:* My body and my environment are made up of atoms, elements, molecules, and compounds. Understanding this will help me understand how my body and the environment work, which will help me to know how to take better care of both.

## R—Recite:

Reread the heading and subheading and look at the questions you asked. First, briefly answer these questions in your own words without looking at the section. Then, look back to see if you are correct.

*What are elements? How are these related to "life" and "energy"?*

Elements are the ninety-two naturally occurring atoms that make up all of the matter on earth. Elements are the "building blocks" of life, which are assembled and disassembled by laws of energy.

*What's the difference between living and nonliving systems?*

Living systems are made up of six key elements: carbon (C), hydrogen (H), oxygen (O), nitrogen (N), phosphorus (P), and sulfur (S). These mainly occur in molecules that are made up primarily of chains of carbon and hydrogen atoms. Nonliving systems are generally inorganic, made up of molecules or compounds with no carbon-carbon bonds.

*What role does energy play in the ecosystem?*

The universe is made up of matter and energy. Matter has mass and occupies space. Energy is the ability to move matter, and is divided into two types: kinetic energy, which is energy in action, and potential energy, which is energy in storage. Energy can be converted from kinetic to potential in many ways. All changes in matter occur by the absorption or release of energy.

### R—Review

Look over the total chapter by rereading the headings and subheadings. Try to answer the question you made from each heading without looking back at what you originally wrote or looking at the text. See if you understand the key ideas (e.g., matter, atoms, elements) that you made note of during the Read stage.

**Activity →** In the textbook chapter in appendix 1, "Ecosystems: How They Work," start on page 55 with the section titled "Energy Considerations" and read through page 59. Using these five pages, work through the following SQ3R worksheet with a partner.

# SQ3R Worksheet

## S—Survey
Read the title of the chapter, the table of contents, the introduction, each boldface heading, summary, and the questions at the end of the chapter.

1. What are these pages about?
2. What topics are included on these pages?
3. How does this textbook help you with this "survey" process?

## Q—Question
Turn the main heading ("Energy Considerations") into at least one question (p. 55) and do the same with the two subheadings ("Matter and Energy," p. 55; "Energy Laws," p. 59). Remember the "wh" questions: Who, what, when, where, why, and how.

Question 1
Question 2
Question 3

## R—Read
Read the material following the heading and the first subheading, looking for the answers to your questions. Think about how the material is organized. Take note of key ideas and other important information. Think about how this information applies to your life. Think about what is difficult to understand and what you can do to help you improve your comprehension.

## R—Recite
Reread the heading and subheading and look at the questions you asked. First, briefly answer these questions in your own words without looking at the section. Then, look back to see if you are correct.

Answer 1
Answer 2

## Q—Question, R—Read, Q—Question, R—Read, etc.
Move to the second subheading and repeat the process.

## R—Review
Look over all the pages you read (pp. 55–59). Try to answer the question you created from each heading without looking back at what you originally wrote or looking at the text.

Answer 1
Answer 2
Answer 3

Check to see if you understand the key ideas that you noted while reading.

## Putting It into Practice

**Part 1.** Continue reading the textbook chapter in appendix 1, "Ecosystems: How They Work." Starting on page 60, use the SQ3R process through page 66, stopping when you reach the next main heading, "Principles of Ecosystem Function." Skip the "Global Perspective" box on page 65 for now. Take notes of what you do for each stage of the SQ3R process. You may find it helpful to use the SQ3R worksheet as a guide.

**Part 2.** Using a textbook that you are reading for an academic class, other materials assigned by your instructor, or the textbook chapter in appendix 2 titled "The Diffusion of Languages," use the SQ3R method to study/read it. Take notes on what you do for each stage of the SQ3R process. You may find it helpful to use the SQ3R worksheet as a guide.

# Chapter 11 TAKING NOTES: THE CORNELL METHOD

Chapter 9 noted that successful academic readers are active, strategic, and metacognitive. Chapter 10 introduced a technique—SQ3R—that encourages active, strategic, metacognitive thinking while you read academic texts. The SQ3R method is a great tool for understanding the general ideas presented in a textbook, which is often all you need to do. However, there are times when you will be required to have a detailed understanding of the material presented in a textbook. This chapter looks at another method, which you can combine with SQ3R, that will help you carefully study the material in a textbook.

Many readers like to highlight or underline information as they read textbooks. Unfortunately, highlighting or underlining information does not usually encourage active thinking. Students who invest the time to take notes on what they are reading, and have a method for organizing their notes, better understand the material that they have read and are likely to do better in their classes.

A popular note-taking method used by many college students was developed at Cornell University for lecture notes. However, it is also very successfully used in taking notes from a textbook.

## Explanation and Examples

The **Cornell method** of note-taking provides a strategy and a structure for making your reading and learning of academic material more efficient and effective. The following steps outline how this method works. The description below assumes you will be writing your notes by hand, but it can easily be modified if you prefer to take your notes on a computer.

### Preparing to Take Notes:

1. Use loose-leaf notebook paper (or word-processing software on your computer).

2. Put the date, name of the chapter, and page numbers in the upper-right-hand corner.

3. Draw a vertical line about 2 ½ inches (6 cm) from the left edge of the paper running from top to bottom. You will take notes to the right of this vertical line; the left column will be used after you read to write key words and phrases that summarize your notes. (If you are using a computer, it probably works best to create a table that has two columns. This way it is easy to move from one column to another and to add information later.)

Your page should look something like this.

| | Date<br>Chapter Title<br>Page #s |
|---|---|
| | |
| | |
| | |
| | |
| | |
| | |

## Taking Notes (Survey, Question, and Read)

1. Using the SQ3R technique discussed in chapter 10, survey the material you will be reading.

2. Focus on determining the *main ideas* for the paragraphs and sections that you are reading. Write the main ideas clearly and completely. Remember the following tips to help you determine the main ideas.

   a. Use strategies discussed in chapter 5 to find main ideas. Ask yourself: What is the writer talking about here? What is it that the writer thinks is important?

   b. Use strategies discussed in chapters 6–8 to determine what organizational patterns the writer is using. For example, if the writer is comparing two things, then you need to clearly indicate in your notes what two things are being compared.

   c. As suggested with the SQ3R method, turn headings and subheadings into questions. When you answer the question, you will probably have the main idea for that section.

3. Include details and examples in reduced form, using single words or short phrases. For example, if the main idea is "The U.S. government is divided into three branches," you could then list the detail as "(1) legislative, (2) executive, (3) judicial."

4. Abbreviate words when possible, but be sure to abbreviate consistently and in a way that you will understand later. For example, some common abbreviations are **&** (*and, as well as*), **w/** (*with*), **w/o** (*without*), **=** (*is, means*), **+** (*and, in addition*), **gov't** (*government*).

5. Be sure to include important words that are introduced and defined. See chapter 2 for a review of how to identify these technical words.

6. If the textbook has a summary or key terms section at the end of the chapter, make sure you include this information in your notes.

7. In some cases, your notes may include diagrams, charts, or drawings if they are necessary in order to understand the main idea. For example, if you are studying cell biology, it may be important to draw a diagram of a cell with its parts labeled.

8. Leave some space after each main idea and every time you come to a new heading or subheading in the text. This allows you to add more information later as you study your notes and also makes them easier to read.

Read the first full page of the textbook chapter in appendix 1, "Ecosystems: How They Work" (p. 52). Notes using the Cornell method will look something like the following.

| | |
|---|---|
| | September 22 |
| | <u>Ecosystems: How They Work</u> |
| | p. 52 |
| | |
| | Elements, Life, and Energy |
| |     What are <u>elements</u>? How are these related to "<u>life</u>" and "<u>energy</u>"? |
| |       * Elements = 92 naturally occurring atoms |
| |         • make up all matter (gases, liquids, solids) on earth |
| |         • "building blocks" of life |
| |         • assembled (growth) and disassembled (decay) by laws of energy |
| |       * Atoms never change or are created/destroyed |
| |         • = Law of Conservation of Matter |
| | |
| | Organization of Elements in Living & Nonliving Systems |
| |     What's the difference between <u>living</u> and <u>nonliving</u> systems? |
| |       * Molecule = any 2 or more bonded atoms ($O_2$) |
| |       * Compound = 2 or more <u>different</u> bonded atoms ($CO_2$) |
| |       * Key elements (atoms) in <u>living systems</u>: |
| |         nitrogen (N) |
| |         carbon (C) |
| |         hydrogen (H)        acronym = N CHOPS |
| |         oxygen (O) |
| |         phosphorus (P) |
| |         sulfur (S) |
| |       * Lower atmosphere contains $O_2$, $N_2$, $CO_2$ |
| |         • air major source of 3 elements for organisms |

**Recite**

After you read a page or two in your text, and always at the end of a major section, take a minute to look over your notes.

1. Make sure you can read and understand what you have written.

2. In the left column next to your notes, write key words that will serve as cues to help you remember the information in the right column. Thinking about and writing these key words helps you to actively process what you have written, and they help you to better remember more information.

   • Key words should be single words if possible, or at most short phrases.
   • Key words should summarize the information in each section.

Using the notes that we took above, our page looks like the following after we have added the key words and phrases to the left column.

| | September 22<br>Ecosystems: How They Work<br>p. 52 |
|---|---|
| Elements | Elements, Life, and Energy<br>    What are <u>elements</u>? How are these related to "<u>life</u>" and "<u>energy</u>"?<br>        * Elements = 92 naturally occurring atoms<br>            • make up all matter (gases, liquids, solids) on earth<br>            • "building blocks" of life<br>            • assembled (growth) and disassembled (decay) by laws of energy |
| Law of Conservation<br>of Matter |        * Atoms never change or are created/destroyed<br>            • = Law of Conservation of Matter |
| Molecule Compound | Organization of Elements in Living & Nonliving Systems<br>    What's the difference between <u>living</u> and <u>nonliving</u> systems?<br>        * Molecule = any 2 or more bonded atoms ($O_2$)<br>        * Compound = 2 or more <u>different</u> bonded atoms ($CO_2$)<br>        * Key elements (atoms) in <u>living systems</u>:<br>            nitrogen (N) |
| Key Elements:<br>N CHOPS |            carbon (C)<br>            hydrogen (H)       acronym = N CHOPS<br>            oxygen (O)<br>            phosphorus (P)<br>            sulfur (S) |
| Key elements in air |        * Lower atmosphere contains $O_2$, $N_2$, $CO_2$<br>            • air major source of 3 elements for organisms |

**Review**

Once you have completed your notes using the Cornell method, you have a great tool for reviewing and studying the material you have read. Cover the right column of your notes so that only the left column with the key words is showing. Look at the key words and try to recite as much information as you can about the topic. Then look at your notes in the right column to check what you remembered. If you review your notes in this manner on a weekly basis, you should be well prepared for a test on the material.

**Activity →**  The following activity uses the chapter in appendix 1, "Ecosystems: How They Work." Read and take notes on pages 55–59 of this chapter, starting with the heading titled "Energy Considerations." Below is the start of notes on this section. Using the steps given above, finish the notes in the right column. Then review what you have written and add key words in the left column. Compare your notes with your classmates' notes.

| | |
|---|---|
| | September 22 <br> <u>Ecosystems: How They Work</u> <br> p. 55–59 |
| Matter | What role does energy play in the ecosystem? <br>   * Universe = matter & energy <br>   * Matter = anything that occupies space and has mass <br>     • solids, liquids, gases <br>     • living & nonliving things <br>     • atoms = basic unit of matter |
| Energy |   * Energy = light, heat, movement, electricity <br>     • no mass, no space <br>     • affects matter <br>       – changes position or state <br>     • = ability to move matter <br>   * Two Types of Energy <br>     1) <u>Kinetic</u> = energy in action or motion <br>       -light, heat energy, physical motion, electricity <br>     2) <u>Potential</u> = energy in storage <br>       -stretched rubber band <br>       -fuels (gasoline, etc.) = chemical energy <br>     • Changing types energy <br>       -potential → kinetic (Fig. 3-8) <br>       -kinetic → potential (charging a battery) <br>   * Measuring Energy |

## Putting It into Practice ▌ ▌ ▌

**Part 1.** Using the SQ3R method and the Cornell method described above, finish taking reading notes on the chapter in appendix 1, "Ecosystems: How They Work," starting with the section "Matter and Energy Changes in Organisms and Ecosystems," on page 60, and going through to the end of the chapter.

**Part 2.** Using a textbook that you are reading for an academic class, other materials assigned to you by your instructor, or the textbook chapter in appendix 2 titled "The Diffusion of Languages," use the SQ3R method to read it. As you read, take complete notes using the Cornell method described above.

# APPENDIXES

# Appendix 1

# CHAPTER 3

# Ecosystems: How They Work

## Key Issues and Questions

1. All the elements that comprise living things come from the environment. What are these key elements? Where is each found?

2. Life processes can be seen in terms of the assembly and disassembly of complex molecules. What molecules are formed in growth? In the breakdown of organic compounds?

3. Changes in matter cannot be separated from changes in energy. Relate inputs and outputs of energy to various changes in matter.

4. Photosynthesis and cell respiration are the two fundamental biological processes. What matter and energy changes occur in these two processes? Relate them to the dynamics of ecosystems.

5. Recycling of elements and flow of energy are fundamental aspects of all ecosystems. Describe specifically how various atoms are recycled in, and how energy flows through, ecosystems.

6. A third fundamental feature of all ecosystems is the biomass pyramid. What three factors make such a pyramid inevitable? What occurs if higher trophic levels are increased?

7. Sustainability of natural ecosystems is supported by three principles. Name these principles. Relate problems regarding sustainability of the human system to these principles.

*I*n this chapter, we explore how ecosystems work at the fundamental level of chemicals and energy. Our look at this basic level will reveal underlying principles that enable natural ecosystems to be sustainable, and it will provide insight into the pathways we must take to make our human system sustainable. Also, understanding at this level will provide a background for understanding agricultural problems, pollution, global warming, and other issues covered in the text.

*Masai Mara National Park, Kenya.* [Photo by M.P. Kahl/Photo Researchers, Inc.]

# Elements, Life, and Energy

The basic building blocks of all **matter** (all gases, liquids, and solids in both living and nonliving systems) are **atoms**. Only 92 different kinds of atoms occur in nature, and these are known as the 92 naturally occurring **elements**. In addition, physicists have created 14 more in the laboratory, but all of these break down again into the naturally occurring elements such as carbon, hydrogen, oxygen, and iron (see Table C-1, p. 639).

How can the innumerable materials that make up our world, including the tissues of living things, be made of just 92 elements? More specifically, 99% of Earth's crust is composed of only eight of these natural elements.

Elements are analogous to Lego® blocks: From a small number of basic kinds of blocks, we can build innumerable different things. Also, like blocks, nature's materials can be taken apart into their separate constituent atoms, and the atoms can then be reassembled into different materials. All chemical reactions, whether they occur in a test tube, in the environment, or inside living things, and whether they occur very slowly or very fast, involve rearrangements of atoms to form different kinds of matter.

Atoms do not change during the disassembly and reassembly of different materials. A carbon atom, for instance, will always remain a carbon atom. Furthermore, atoms are not created or destroyed during any chemical reactions. This constancy of atoms is regarded as a fundamental natural law, the *law of conservation of matter.*

On the chemical level, then, the cycle of growth, reproduction, death, and decay of organisms can be seen as a continuous process of taking various atoms from the environment, assembling them into living organisms (growth) and then disassembling them (decay) and repeating the process. Of course, in nature, there is no one visible doing the assembling and disassembling; it occurs according to the atoms' chemical nature and to flows of energy. Nonetheless, the simplicity of the concept does not diminish the wonder of it.

Which atoms make up living organisms? Where are they found in the environment? How do they become part of living organisms? We answer these questions next.

## Organization of Elements in Living and Nonliving Systems

A more detailed discussion of atoms—how they differ from one another, how they bond to form various gases, liquids, and solids, and how we use chemical formulas to describe different chemicals—is given in Appendix C (page 639). Studying that appendix first may give you a better comprehension of the material we are about to cover. At the very least, the definitions of two terms are essential: *molecule* and *compound.*

A **molecule** refers to *any* two or more atoms bonded together in a specific way. The properties of a material are dependent on the specific way in which atoms are bonded to form molecules as well as on the atoms themselves. Similarly, a **compound** refers to any *two or more different kinds* of atoms bonded together. Note the distinction that a molecule may consist of two or more of the *same kind*, as well as different kinds, of atoms bonded together. A compound always implies that at least two different kinds of atoms are involved. For example, the fundamental units of oxygen gas, which consist of two oxygen atoms bonded together, are molecules but not a compound. Water, on the other hand, can be referred to as either molecules or a compound, since the fundamental units are two hydrogen atoms bonded to an oxygen atom. Some further distinctions are given in Appendix C.

The key elements in living systems (and their chemical symbols) are carbon (C), hydrogen (H), oxygen (O), nitrogen (N), phosphorus (P), and sulfur (S). You can remember them by the acronym N. CHOPS. These six elements are the building blocks of all the organic molecules that make up the tissues of plants, animals, and microbes. We have said that growth and decay can be seen as a process of atoms moving from the environment into living things and returning to the environment. By looking at the chemical nature of air, water, and minerals, we shall see where our six key elements and others occur in the environment (Table 3-1).

The lower atmosphere is a mixture of molecules of three important gases—oxygen ($O_2$), nitrogen ($N_2$), and carbon dioxide ($CO_2$)—along with trace amounts of several other gases that have no immediate biological importance. Also generally present in air are variable amounts of polluting materials and water vapor. The three main gases found in air are shown in Figure 3-1. Note three of the key elements among these molecules. Thus, air is a source of carbon, oxygen, and nitrogen for all organisms.

**TABLE 3-1**

## Elements Found in Living Organisms and Locations in the Environment

| Element (Kind of Atom) | Symbol | Biologically Important Molecule or Ion in Which the Element Occurs[a] | | Location in the Environment | | |
|---|---|---|---|---|---|---|
| | | Name | Formula | Air | Dissolved in Water | Some Rock and Soil Minerals |
| Carbon | C | Carbon dioxide | $CO_2$ | X | X | X($CO_3^-$) |
| Hydrogen | H | Water | $H_2O$ | | (Water itself) | |
| Atomic oxygen (required in respiration) | O | Oxygen gas | $O_2$ | X | X | |
| Molecular oxygen (released in photosynthesis) | $O_2$ | Water | $H_2O$ | | (Water itself) | |
| Nitrogen | N | Nitrogen gas | $N_2$ | X | X | Via fixation |
| | | Ammonium ion | $NH_4^+$ | | X | X |
| | | Nitrate ion | $NO_3^-$ | | X | X |
| Sulfur | S | Sulfate ion | $SO_4^{2-}$ | | X | X |
| Phosphorus | P | Phosphate ion | $PO_4^{3-}$ | | X | X |
| Potassium | K | Potassium ion | $K^+$ | | X | X |
| Calcium | Ca | Calcium ion | $Ca^{2+}$ | | X | X |
| Magnesium | Mg | Magnesium ion | $Mg^{2+}$ | | X | X |
| *Trace Elements*[b] | | | | | | |
| Iron | Fe | Iron ion | $Fe^{2+}, Fe^{3+}$ | | X $Fe^{2+}$ only | X |
| Manganese | Mn | Manganese ion | $Mn^{2+}$ | | X | X |
| Boron | B | Boron ion | $B^{3+}$ | | X | X |
| Zinc | Zn | Zinc ion | $Zn^{2+}$ | | X | X |
| Copper | Cu | Copper ion | $Cu^{2+}$ | | X | X |
| Molybdenum | Mo | Molybdenum ion | $Mo^{2+}$ | | X | X |
| Chlorine | Cl | Chloride ion | $Cl^-$ | | X | X |

NOTE: These elements are found in *all* living organisms—plants, animals, and microbes. Some organisms require certain elements in addition to the ones given. For example, humans require sodium and iodine.

[a] A molecule is a chemical unit of two or more atoms bonded together. An ion is a single atom or group of bonded atoms that has acquired a positive or negative charge as indicated.

[b] Only small or trace amounts of these elements are required.

Saying that air is a **mixture** means that there is no chemical bonding between the molecules involved. Indeed, it is this lack of connection between molecules that results in air being gaseous. Attraction, or bonding, between molecules results in liquid or solid states.

The source of the key element hydrogen is water. Each molecule of water consists of two hydrogen atoms bonded to an oxygen atom, as indicated by the formula for water: $H_2O$. A weak attraction between water molecules is known as *hydrogen bonding*. At temperatures below freezing, hydrogen bonding holds the molecules in position with respect to one another, and the result is a solid (ice or snow). At temperatures above freezing, but below vaporization (evaporation), hydrogen bonding still holds the molecules close, but allows them to move around one another, producing the liquid state. Vaporization occurs as hydrogen bonds break and

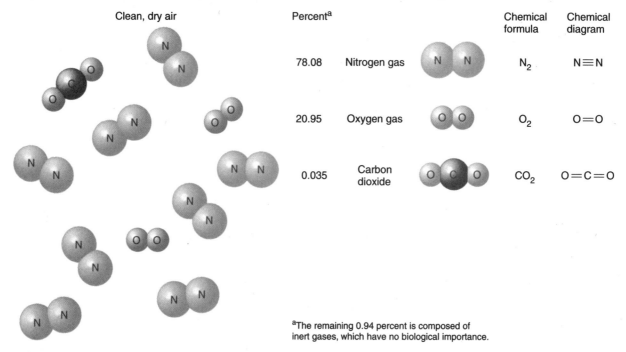

**Clean, dry air is a mixture of molecules of three important gases.**

| Clean, dry air | Percent[a] | | | Chemical formula | Chemical diagram |
|---|---|---|---|---|---|
| | 78.08 | Nitrogen gas | | $N_2$ | N≡N |
| | 20.95 | Oxygen gas | | $O_2$ | O=O |
| | 0.035 | Carbon dioxide | | $CO_2$ | O=C=O |

[a]The remaining 0.94 percent is composed of inert gases, which have no biological importance.

**FIGURE 3-1**

From a biological point of view, the three most important gases of the lower atmosphere are nitrogen, oxygen, and carbon dioxide.

water molecules move into the air independently. With a lowering of temperature, all these changes in state go in the reverse direction (Fig. 3-2). We reemphasize that, regardless of the changes in state, the water molecules themselves retain their basic structure of two hydrogen atoms bonded to an oxygen atom. It is only the relationship between the molecules that changes.

All the other elements required by living organisms, as well as the 72 or so elements that are not required, are found in various rock and soil minerals. A **mineral** refers to any hard, crystalline, inorganic material of a given chemical composition. Most rocks are made up of relatively small crystals of two or more minerals, and soil generally consists of particles of many different minerals. Each mineral is made up of dense clusters of two or more kinds of atoms bonded together by an attraction between positive and negative charges on the atoms as explained in Appendix C and Fig. 3-3.

There are simple but significant interactions between air, water, and minerals. Gases from the air and ions (charged atoms) from minerals may dissolve in water. Therefore, natural water is inevitably a *solution* containing variable amounts of dissolved gases and minerals. This solution is constantly subject to change, as any dissolved substances may be removed from it by various processes, or additional materials may dissolve in it. Molecules of water enter the air by evaporation

and leave it by means of condensation and precipitation. (See the water cycle, p. 264). Thus, the amount of moisture in air is constantly fluctuating. Wind may carry a certain amount of dust or mineral particles, and this amount is also changing constantly, since the particles gradually settle out from the air. The various interactions are summarized in Fig. 3-4.

By contrast to the relatively simple molecules that occur in the environment (for example, $CO_2$, $H_2O$, $N_2$), in living organisms we find the key atoms (C, H, O, N, P, S) bonded into very large, complex molecules known as proteins, carbohydrates (sugars and starches), lipids (fatty substances), and nucleic acids. Some of these molecules may contain millions of atoms, and their potential diversity is infinite. Indeed, the diversity of living things is a reflection of the diversity of such molecules.

The molecules that make up the tissues of living things are constructed mainly from carbon atoms bonded together into chains with hydrogen atoms attached. Oxygen, nitrogen, phosphorus, and sulfur may be present also, but the key common denominator is carbon-carbon and/or carbon-hydrogen bonds (Fig. 3-5). Recall (page 28) that material making up the tissues of living organisms is referred to as *organic*. Hence, these *carbon-based molecules, which make up the tissues of living organisms*, are called **organic mol-**

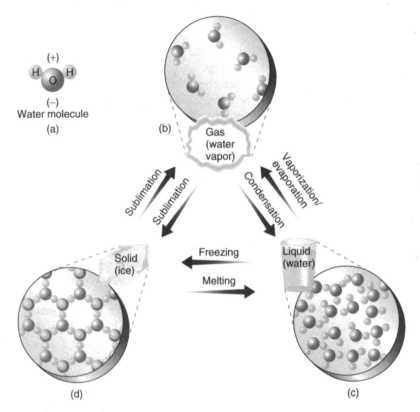

**(a)**
(+)
H — O — H
(−)
Water molecule
(a)

**(b)**
Gas
(water
vapor)

Sublimation

Sublimation

Condensation

Vaporization/
evaporation

Freezing

Melting

Solid
(ice)

Liquid
(water)

(d)

(c)

**FIGURE 3-2**
(a) Water consists of molecules, each of which is formed by two hydrogen atoms bonded to an oxygen atom ($H_2O$). (b) In water vapor, the molecules are separate and independent. (c) In liquid water, the weak attraction between water molecules known as hydrogen bonding gives the water its liquid property. (d) At freezing temperatures, hydrogen bonding holds the molecules firmly, giving the solid state—ice. (After Robert Christopherson, *Geosystems*, 2/e. ©1994, p. 186. Adapted by permission of Prentice Hall, Upper Saddle River, New Jersey. After B.J. Nebel, *Environmental Science*, 2/e. ©1987, p. 46. Prentice Hall, Upper Saddle River, New Jersey.)

**ecules**. (Don't miss the similarity between the words *organic* and *organism*.) **Inorganic**, then, refers to molecules or compounds with neither carbon-carbon nor carbon-hydrogen bonds.

Causing some confusion is the fact that all plastics and countless other human-made compounds are based on carbon-carbon bonding and are, chemically speaking, organic compounds—although they have nothing to do with living systems. Where there is doubt, we resolve this confusion by referring to the compounds of living

organisms as **natural organic compounds** and the human-made ones as **synthetic organic compounds**.

In conclusion, we can see that the elements essential to life (C, H, O, and so on) are present in air, water, or minerals in relatively simple molecules. In living *organ*isms, on the other hand, they are *organ*ized into very complex *organ*ic molecules. These organic compounds in turn make up the various parts of cells, which make up the tissues and organs of the body (Fig. 3-6). Growth, then, may be seen as using the atoms from simple molecules in the environment to construct the complex organic molecules of an organism. Decomposition and decay may be seen as the reverse process. We shall look at each of these processes in more detail later in the chapter; first, however, we must consider another factor: *energy*.

## Energy Considerations

In addition to the rearrangement of atoms, chemical reactions also involve the absorption or release of energy. To grasp this concept, let us examine the distinction between matter and energy.

**Matter and Energy.** The universe is made up of *matter* and *energy*. A more technical definition of **matter** than the one given earlier in this chapter is, *anything that occupies space and has mass*—that is, can

**FIGURE 3-3**
Minerals (hard crystalline compounds) are composed of dense clusters of atoms of two or more elements. The atoms of most elements gain or lose one or more electrons, becoming negative (−) or positive (+) ions. The ions are held together by an attraction between positive and negative charges.

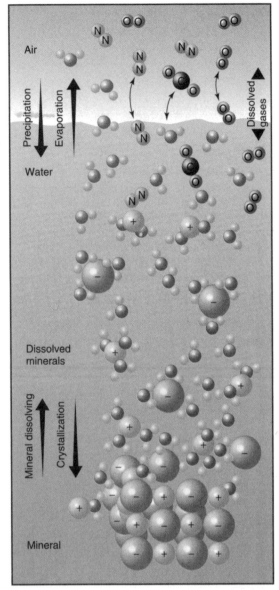

**FIGURE 3-4**
Interrelationship among air, water, and minerals. Minerals and gases dissolve in water, forming solutions. Water evaporates into air, causing humidity. These processes are all reversible: Minerals in solution recrystallize, and water vapor in the air condenses to form liquid water.

*Light, heat, movement,* and *electricity,* on the other hand, do not have mass, nor do they occupy space. (Note that heat, as used here, refers not to a hot object but to the heat energy we can feel radiating from the hot object.) These are the common forms of *energy* which we experience continually—or perhaps their lack is a more significant experience. What do forms of energy have in common? They *affect* matter, causing changes in its *position* or its *state.* For example, the release of energy in an explosion causes things to go flying, a change in position. Heating water causes it to boil and change to steam, a change in state. On a molecular level, changes in state may be seen as movements of atoms or molecules. For example, the degree of heat energy is actually a measure of the relative vibrational motion of the atoms and molecules of the substance. Therefore, **energy** is the ability to move matter.

Energy is commonly divided into two major categories: *kinetic* and *potential* (Fig. 3-7). **Kinetic energy** is *energy in action or motion.* Light, heat energy, physical motion, and electrical current are all forms of kinetic energy. **Potential energy** is energy in storage. A substance or system with potential energy has the capacity, or *potential,* to release one or more forms of kinetic energy. A stretched rubber band, for example, has potential energy; it can send a paper clip flying. Numerous chemicals, such as gasoline and other fuels, release kinetic energy—heat energy, light, and movement—when ignited. The potential energy contained in such chemicals and fuels is called **chemical energy**.

Energy may be changed from one form to another in innumerable ways. How many examples can you think of in addition to those shown in Fig. 3-8? Besides seeing that potential energy may be converted to kinetic

**FIGURE 3-5**
The organic molecules making up living organisms are larger and more complex than the inorganic molecules found in the environment. Glucose and cystine show this relative complexity. (Do *not* memorize these formulas; they are here just to give you a sense of the complexity we are describing.)

$$
\begin{array}{c}
\quad\text{O}\ \ \text{OH}\ \text{H}\ \ \text{OH}\ \text{OH}\ \ \text{H} \\
\quad\|\ \ \ |\ \ \ |\ \ \ \ |\ \ \ |\ \ \ \ | \\
\text{H}-\text{C}-\text{C}-\text{C}-\text{C}-\text{C}-\text{C}-\text{H} \\
\quad\ \ |\ \ \ |\ \ \ |\ \ \ |\ \ \ | \\
\quad\ \ \text{H}\ \ \text{OH}\ \ \text{H}\ \ \ \text{H}\ \ \text{OH}
\end{array}
$$

Glucose, a sugar

$$
\begin{array}{c}
\quad\ \ \ \text{H}\ \ \ \text{H}\ \ \ \text{O} \\
\quad\ \ \ |\ \ \ \ |\ \ \ \ \| \\
\text{HS}-\text{C}-\text{C}-\text{C}-\text{OH} \\
\quad\ \ \ |\ \ \ \ | \\
\quad\ \ \ \text{H}\ \ \text{NH}_2
\end{array}
$$

Cystine, an amino acid occurring in proteins

be weighed when gravity is present. This definition obviously covers all solids, liquids, and gases, and living as well as nonliving things.

Atoms are made up of protons, neutrons, and electrons, which in turn are made of still smaller particles. Thus, physicists debate what the most basic unit of matter is. However, since atoms are the basic units of all elements and remain unchanged during chemical reactions, it is practical to consider them as the basic units of matter.

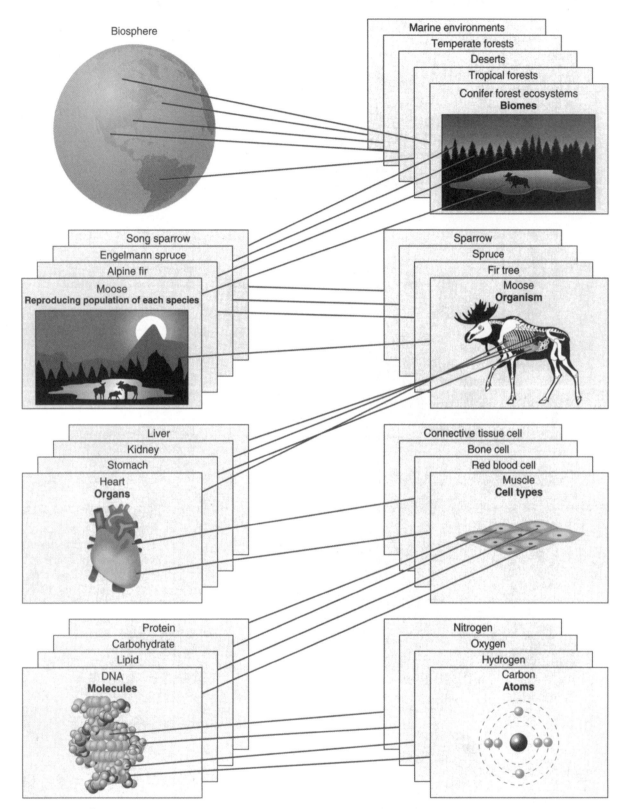

**FIGURE 3-6**

Life can be seen as a hierarchy of organization of matter. In the inorganic sphere, elements are arranged simply in molecules of the air, water, and minerals. In living organisms, they are arranged in very complex organic molecules, which, in turn, make up cells that constitute tissues, organs, and, thus, the whole organism. Levels of organization continue up through populations, species, ecosystems, and, finally, the whole biosphere.

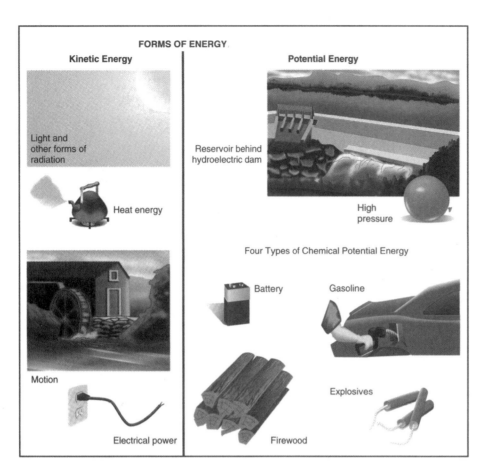

**FORMS OF ENERGY**

**Kinetic Energy**

Light and other forms of radiation

Heat energy

Motion

Electrical power

**Potential Energy**

Reservoir behind hydroelectric dam

High pressure

Four Types of Chemical Potential Energy

Battery

Gasoline

Explosives

Firewood

**FIGURE 3-7**

Energy is distinct from matter in that energy neither has mass nor occupies space. It has the ability to act on matter, changing the position of the matter and/or its state. Kinetic energy is energy in one of its active forms. Potential energy refers to systems or materials that have the potential to release kinetic energy. In this text, we use the term *heat energy* to refer to thermal infrared energy.

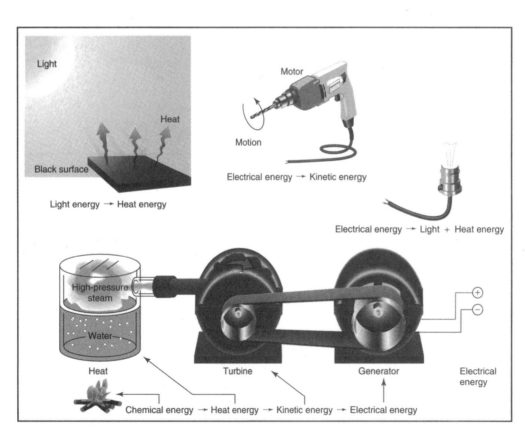

Light

Heat

Black surface

Light energy → Heat energy

Motor

Motion

Electrical energy → Kinetic energy

Electrical energy → Light + Heat energy

High-pressure steam

Water

Heat

Turbine

Generator

Electrical energy

Chemical energy → Heat energy → Kinetic energy → Electrical energy

**FIGURE 3-8**

Any form of energy can be converted to any other form, except that heat energy can be transferred only to something cooler. Heat is a form of energy that flows from one system or object to another because the two are at different temperatures.

energy, it is especially important to recognize that kinetic energy may be converted to potential energy, as in charging a battery or pumping water into a high-elevation reservoir. We shall see shortly that photosynthesis is another such process.

Because energy does not have mass or occupy space, it cannot be measured in units of weight or volume, but it can be measured in other kinds of units. One of the most common units is the **calorie**, which is defined as the *amount of heat required to raise the temperature of 1 gram (1 milliliter) of water 1 degree Celsius*. Since this is a very small unit, it is frequently more convenient to speak in terms of kilocalories (1 kilocalorie = 1,000 calories), the amount of heat required to raise 1 liter (1000 milliliters) of water 1 degree Celsius. Kilocalories are sometimes denoted as "Calories" with a capital "C." Food Calories, which are a measure of how much energy our bodies can derive from given foods, are actually kilocalories. Any form of energy can be measured in calories by converting it to heat energy and measuring that heat in terms of a rise in the temperature of water. Temperature is a measurement of the molecular motion in a substance caused by the kinetic energy present.

We define energy as the ability to move matter. Conversely, no change in the movement of matter can occur *without* the absorption or release of energy. Indeed, no change in matter—from a few atoms joining together or coming apart in a chemical reaction to a major volcanic eruption—can be separated from respective changes in energy.

**Energy Laws: Laws of Thermodynamics.** Knowing that energy can be converted from one form to another has led numerous would-be inventors over the years to try to build machines or devices that would produce more energy than they consumed. A common idea that occurs to many students is to use the output from a generator to drive a motor that, in turn, drives the generator to keep the cycle going and yields additional power in the bargain. Unfortunately, all such devices have one feature in common: They don't work. When all the inputs and outputs of energy are carefully measured, they are found to be *equal*. There is no net gain or loss in total energy. This observation is now accepted as a fundamental natural law, **the law of conservation of energy**, also called the **first law of thermodynamics:** *Energy is neither created nor destroyed, but may be converted from one form to another.* The law is also commonly stated as "You can't get something for nothing."

Fanciful "energy generators" fail for two reasons: First, in every energy conversion, a portion of the energy is converted to heat energy (thermal infrared).

Second, heat always flows toward cooler surroundings. There is no way of trapping and recycling heat energy, since it can flow only "downhill" toward a cooler place. Consequently, in the absence of energy inputs, any and every system will sooner or later come to a stop as its energy is converted to heat and lost. This is now accepted as another natural law, the **second law of thermodynamics**. Basically, the second law says that, *in any energy conversion, you will end up with* less *usable energy than you started with.* So, not only can you not get something for nothing (the first law), you can't even break even.

A principle that underlies the loss of heat is the principle of increasing *entropy*. **Entropy** refers to the degree of *disorder: Increasing entropy means increasing disorder.* The principle is that, without energy inputs, everything goes in one direction only: toward increasing entropy. This principle of ever-increasing entropy is most readily apparent in the fact that all human-made things tend to deteriorate. We never observe the reverse—a run-down building renovating itself, for example. Students often like to speak of the increasing disorder of their dormitory rooms as the semester wears on as an example of entropy.

The conversion of energy and the loss of heat are both aspects of increasing entropy. Heat energy is the result of the random vibrational motion of atoms and molecules. Thus, it is the lowest (most disordered) form of energy, and its flow to cooler surroundings is a way for that disorder to spread. Therefore, the second law of thermodynamics is nowadays more generally stated as: *Systems will go spontaneously in one direction only; toward increasing entropy.* The second law also says that systems will go spontaneously only toward *lower* potential energy, a direction that releases heat from the systems. (Fig. 3-9).

Very important in the statement of the second law is the word *spontaneously*. It is possible to pump water uphill, charge a battery, stretch a rubber band, compress air, or otherwise increase the potential energy of some system. However, inherent in such words as *pump, charge, stretch*, and *compress* is the fact that energy is being put into the system; in contrast, the opposite direction, which releases energy, occurs spontaneously.

The conclusion is that whenever you see something gaining potential energy, you should realize that that energy is being obtained from somewhere else (the first law). Moreover, the amount of energy lost from that somewhere else is greater than the amount gained (the second law). Let us now relate these concepts of matter and energy to organic molecules, organisms, ecosystems, and the biosphere.

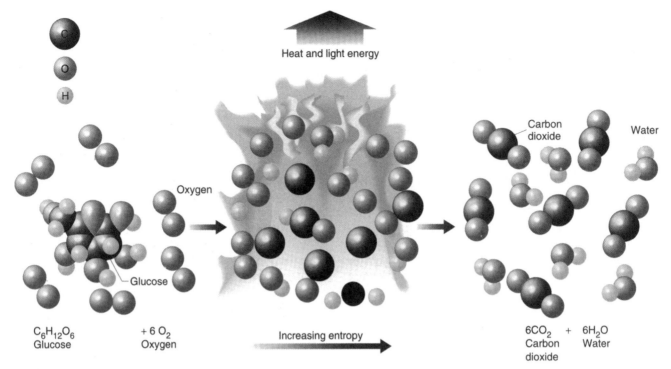

**FIGURE 3-9**
Systems go spontaneously only in the direction of increasing entropy. When glucose, the building-block molecule of wood, is burned, heat is released, and the atoms become more and more disordered, both aspects of increasing entropy. The fact that wood will burn but not form spontaneously is an example of the second law of thermodynamics.

## Matter and Energy Changes in Organisms and Ecosystems

All organic molecules, which make up the tissues of living organisms, contain *high potential energy*. This is evident from the simple fact that they burn: The heat and light of the flame are their potential energy being released as kinetic energy. On the other hand, try as you might, you will not be able to get energy by burning inorganic molecules, such as carbon dioxide, water, or mineral compounds that occur in nature. Indeed, many of these materials are used as fire extinguishers. This extreme nonflammability is evidence that such materials have very *low potential energy*. Thus, the production of organic material from inorganic material involves a *gain* in potential energy. Conversely, the breakdown of organic matter involves a *release* of energy.

In this relationship between the formation and breakdown of organic matter and the gain and release of energy, we can see the energy dynamics of ecosystems. Producers (green plants) play the role of making high-potential-energy organic molecules for their bodies from low-potential-energy raw materials in the environment—namely, carbon dioxide, water, and a few dissolved compounds of nitrogen, phosphorus, and other elements. Such "uphill" conversion is made possible by the light energy absorbed by chlorophyll. On the other hand, all consumers, detritus feeders, and decomposers obtain their energy requirement for movement and other body functions from feeding on and breaking down organic matter (Fig. 3-10). Let us now look at this energy flow in somewhat more detail for each category of organisms.

**Producers.** Recall from Chapter 2 that producers are green plants, which use light energy in the process of *photosynthesis* to make sugar (glucose, stored chemical energy) from carbon dioxide and water and release oxygen gas as a by-product. The process is expressed by the following formula:

PHOTOSYNTHESIS

$$6\ CO_2 \quad + \quad 6\ H_2O \quad \longrightarrow \quad C_6H_{12}O_6 \quad + \quad 6\ O_2$$

carbon dioxide (gas)      water           glucose         oxygen (gas)

(low potential energy)                (high potential energy)

The kinetic energy of light is absorbed by chlorophyll in the cells of the plant and used to remove the hydrogen atoms from water ($H_2O$) molecules. The hydrogen atoms are transferred to carbon atoms coming from carbon dioxide as the carbons are joined in a chain to begin forming a glucose molecule. After the removal of hydrogen from water, the oxygen atoms that remain combine with each other to form oxygen gas, which is released into the air.

Each molecule of glucose is constructed from 6 carbon atoms, 12 hydrogen atoms, and 6 oxygen atoms—hence its formula, $C_6H_{12}O_6$. Thus, the construction of one molecule of glucose requires 6 molecules of carbon dioxide to provide the 6 carbon atoms and 6 molecules of water to provide the 12 hydrogen atoms. Among these molecules of carbon dioxide and water are 18 oxygen atoms, but only 6 are needed. The extra oxygen atoms are given off as molecules of oxygen gas ($O_2$), 6 molecules for every molecule of glucose formed. This accounting, based on careful quantitative measurements, supports the law of conservation of matter. Note that oxygen gas, which is essential for the respiration of animals, is a *waste product* of photosynthesis.

The key energy steps in photosynthesis are removing the hydrogen from water molecules and joining carbon atoms together to form the high-potential-energy carbon-carbon and carbon-hydrogen bonds of glucose in place of the low-potential-energy bonds in water and carbon dioxide molecules. But the laws of thermodynamics are not violated or even strained in this process. Careful measurements show that the rate of photosynthesis (which determines the amount of glucose formed) is proportional to the intensity of light, and only 2–5 calories' worth of sugar is formed for each 100 calories' worth of light energy falling on the plant. Thus, plants are not particularly efficient "machines" in performing this conversion of light energy to chemical energy.

The glucose produced in photosynthesis plays three roles in the plant. First, either by itself or along

**FIGURE 3-10**

Storage and release of potential energy. (a) A simple physical example of the storage and release of potential energy. With suitable energy input, water can be pumped to a higher elevation, thus capturing a portion of the energy input. A portion of the potential energy can then be harnessed to do useful work by letting the water flow back to low potential energy over a turbine. (b) The same principle applies to ecosystems. Through photosynthesis, light energy builds up elements from a low-potential-energy state in inorganic materials to a high-potential-energy state in the form of molecules in organic materials. The breakdown of these molecules releases the energy, which then drives all the active functions of organisms.

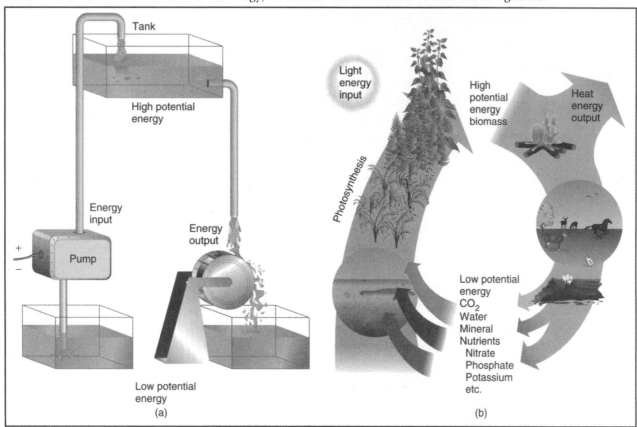

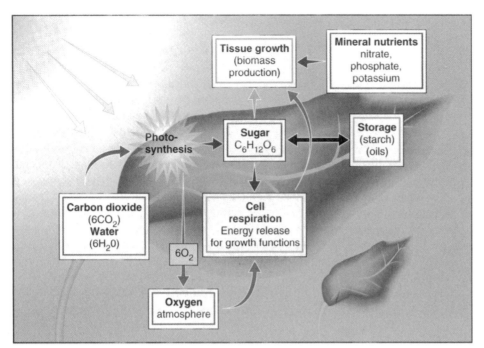

**FIGURE 3-11**
Producers are remarkable chemical factories. Using light energy from the Sun, they make glucose from carbon dioxide and water, releasing oxygen as a byproduct. Breaking down some of the glucose to provide additional chemical energy, they combine the remaining glucose with certain nutrients from the soil to form other complex organic molecules that the plant then uses for growth.

with nitrogen, phosphorus, sulfur, and other mineral nutrients absorbed from the soil or water surrounding the plant's roots, glucose is the raw material used for making all the other organic molecules (proteins, carbohydrates, and so on) that make up the stems, roots, leaves, flowers, and fruits of the plant. Second, the synthesis of all these organic molecules requires additional energy, as does the plant's absorption of nutrients from the soil and certain other functions. This energy is provided when the plant breaks down a portion of the glucose to release its stored energy in a process called *cell respiration,* which will be discussed shortly. Third, a portion of the glucose produced may be stored for future use. For storage, the glucose is generally converted to starch, as in potatoes, or to oils, as in seeds. These conversions are summarized in Fig. 3-11.

**Consumers and Other Heterotrophs—*Energy of Food.*** Obviously, consumers need energy to move about and to perform such bodily functions as pumping blood. In addition, consumers need energy to synthesize all the molecules required for growth, maintenance, and repair of the body. Where does this energy come from? It comes from the breakdown of organic molecules of food (or of the body's own tissues if food is not available). About 60–90 percent of the food that we or other consumers eat and digest acts as "fuel" to provide energy.

First, the starches, fats, and proteins that you eat are digested in the stomach and/or intestine, which means that they are broken into simpler molecules—starches into sugar (glucose), for example. These simpler molecules are then absorbed from the intestine

into the bloodstream and transported to individual cells of the body.

Inside each cell, organic molecules may be broken down through a process called **cell respiration** to release the energy required for the work done by that cell. Most commonly, cell respiration involves the breakdown of glucose, and the overall chemistry is the reverse of that for photosynthesis:

CELL RESPIRATION
(An energy-releasing process)

$$C_6H_{12}O_6 \; + \; 6\,O_2 \; \longrightarrow \; 6\,CO_2 \; + \; 6\,H_2O$$

glucose     oxygen     energy released     carbon dioxide     water

(high potential energy)     (low potential energy)

Again, the key point of cell respiration is to release the potential energy contained in organic molecules to perform the activities of the organism. However, other aspects of the chemistry are also significant. Note that oxygen is *released* in photosynthesis, but in cell respiration it is *used* to complete the breakdown of glucose to carbon dioxide and water. Oxygen is absorbed through the lungs with every inhalation (or through the gills, in the case of fish) and is transported to all cells via the circulatory system. Carbon dioxide, which is formed as a waste product, moves from the cells into the circulatory system and is eliminated through the lungs (or gills) with every exhalation. The other byproduct, water, serves any of the body's needs for water, which reduces the need to drink water. A number of desert animals, which are adapted to conserve water, do not need to drink any water because that produced by cell respiration is sufficient. However, the bodies of most animals, including ourselves, are less conserving of water; therefore, drinking additional water is necessary. Such water loss from a plant is called *transpiration*.

Again in keeping with the laws of thermodynamics, the energy conversions involved in the body's using the potential energy from glucose to do work are not 100 percent efficient. Considerable waste heat is produced, and this is the source of body heat. This heat output can be measured in cold-blooded animals and in plants, as well as in warm-blooded animals. It is more noticeable in warm-blooded animals only because they produce extra heat, via cell respiration, to maintain their warm-body temperature.

The basis of weight gain or loss should become evident here also. Organic matter is broken down in cell respiration only as it is needed to meet the energy demands of the body; this is why your breathing rate, the outer reflection of cell respiration, varies with changes in your level of exercise and activity. If you consume more calories from food than your body needs, the excess is converted to fat and stored, and the result is a gain in weight. Conversely, the principle of dieting is to eat less and exercise more, to create an energy demand that exceeds the amount of energy contained in the food being consumed. This imbalance forces the body to break down its own tissues to make up the difference, and the result is a weight loss. Of course, carried to an extreme, this imbalance leads to *starvation* and death when the body runs out of anything expendable to break down for its energy needs.

The overall reaction for cell respiration is the same as that for simply burning glucose. Thus, it is not uncommon to speak of "burning" our food for energy. Such a breakdown of molecules is also called **oxidation**. The distinction between burning and cell respiration is that in cell respiration the oxidation takes place in about 20 small steps, so that the energy is released in small "packets" suitable for driving the functions of each cell. If all the energy from glucose molecules were released in a single "bang," as occurs in burning, it would be like heating and lighting a room with large firecrackers—energy, yes, but hardly useful energy.

We have learned that in addition to containing carbon and hydrogen, many organic molecules contain nitrogen, phosphorus, sulfur, and other elements. When such molecules are broken down in cell respiration, the waste byproducts include compounds of nitrogen, phosphorus, and any other elements present, in addition to the usual carbon dioxide and water. These byproducts are excreted in the urine (or as similar waste in other kinds of animals) and returned to the environment, where they may be reabsorbed by plants (Fig. 3-12). Here you can see the movement of elements

**FIGURE 3-12**
Animal wastes are plant fertilizer. When consumers burn food to obtain energy, the waste products are the inorganic nutrients needed by plants. Here, dog urine has been deposited on a lawn. The ring of dark green grass is where the urine has been diluted to optimal concentration; the grass in the center has been killed by overfertilization with concentrated urine. (Photograph by BJN.)

in a cycle between the environment and living organisms. We expand on these cycles shortly.

Also, you can visualize a flow of energy that enters as light and exits as heat. Finally, recall the *biomass pyramid* (Fig. 2-14). At each trophic level, the amount of biomass inevitably decreases by the amount that is oxidized to provide energy for the consuming organisms.

*Nutritive Role of Food.* Whereas 60–90 percent of the food that consumers eat, digest, and absorb is oxidized for energy, the remaining 10–40 percent, which is converted to the body tissues of the consumer, is no less important. This is the fraction that enables the body to grow, as well as to maintain and repair itself.

Carbohydrates (sugars and starches), and fats can be oxidized easily by the body to provide energy. Body growth, maintenance, and repair, however, require particular nutrients—namely, the various vitamins, minerals, and proteins—that are not present in carbohydrates or fats. If any one or more of the specific nutrients is absent from the diet, various diseases associated with **malnutrition** will develop. Thus arises the problem of overconsumption of highly processed "junk foods" such as potato chips, sodas, candies, various baked goods, and alcohol. Rich in fat or sugar or both, these items are very high in calories, but they contain little or none of the necessary nutrients. Consequently, a diet high in

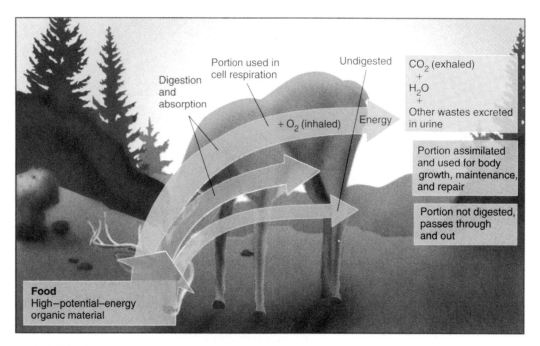

**FIGURE 3-13**

Consumers. Only a small portion of the food ingested by a consumer is assimilated into body growth, maintenance, and repair. A larger amount is used in cell respiration to provide energy for assimilation, movements, and other functions; waste products are carbon dioxide, water, and various mineral nutrients. A third portion is not digested, but instead passes through, becoming fecal waste.

such items may easily oversupply calories and under supply essential nutrients, causing a weight gain and serious disorders of malnutrition at the same time. Yes, many fat people are also malnourished.

***Material Consumed, but Not Digested.*** A portion of what is ingested by consumers is not digested (broken down so that it can be absorbed), but simply passes through the digestive system and out as fecal wastes. For consumers that eat plants, such waste is largely the material of plant cell walls, **cellulose**. We often refer to it as *fiber, bulk,* or *roughage.* Some fiber is a necessary part of the diet in order for the intestines to have something to push through to keep clean and open.

In summary, organic material (food) eaten by any consumer follows one of three pathways: (1) More than 60 percent of what is digested and absorbed is oxidized to provide energy, and waste byproducts are released back to the environment; (2) the remainder of what is digested and absorbed goes into body growth, mainte-nance and repair, or storage (fat); and (3) the portion that is not digested or absorbed passes out as fecal waste (Fig. 3-13). Recognize that in an ecosystem, it is only that portion of the food that becomes body tissue of the con-sumer that becomes food for the next organism in the food chain. Of course, the still-organic fecal waste becomes food for detritus feeders and/or decomposers.

**Detritus Feeders and Decomposers—The Detritivores.** Recall that detritus is mostly dead leaves, the woody parts of plants, and animal fecal wastes. As such, it is largely cellulose, which is unusable by most consumers because they are unable to digest it. Nevertheless, it is still organic and high in potential energy for those organisms that can digest it—namely, the decomposers we learned about in Chapter 2, various species of fungi and bacteria, and a few other microbes. Beyond having this ability to digest cellulose, decomposers act as any other consumer, using the cel-lulose as a source of both energy and nutrients. Termites and some other detritus feeders can digest woody material by virtue of maintaining decomposer microorganisms in their guts in a mutualistic symbiotic relationship. The termite (a detritus feeder) provides a cozy home for the microbes (decomposers) and takes in the cellulose, which the microbes digest for both their own and the termites' benefit.

Most decomposers make use of cell respiration. Thus, the detritus is broken down to carbon dioxide, water, and mineral nutrients. Likewise, there is a release of waste heat, which you may observe as the "steam-ing" of a manure or compost pile on a cold day.

Some decomposers (certain bacteria and yeasts) can meet their energy needs through the partial oxida-tion of glucose that can occur in the absence of oxygen. This modified form of cell respiration is called **fer-mentation**. It results in such end products as ethyl alcohol ($C_2H_6O$), methane gas ($CH_4$), and vinegar (acetic acid, $C_2H_4O_2$). The commercial production of

# Light and Nutrients, the Controlling Factors in Marine Ecosystems

Even though running on solar energy and recycling nutrients are basic principles of sustainability, they are limiting factors in some ecosystems. Indeed, although the availability of moisture is a primary determining factor in terrestrial ecosystems, the availability of light and/or nutrients is a primary determining factor in marine ecosystems.

First, light gets dimmer and dimmer as water depth increases because even clear water absorbs light to some extent. The layer of water from the surface down to the greatest depth at which there is adequate light for photosynthesis is known as the **euphotic zone**. Below the euphotic zone, by definition, photosynthesis does not occur. In clear water, the euphotic zone may be as deep as 600 feet (200 meters), but in very turbid (cloudy) water, it may be a matter of only a few centimeters. If the euphotic zone extends to the bottom, the bottom may support abundant plant life—that is, aquatic vegetation attached to or rooted in the bottom sediments. If the euphotic zone does not extend to the bottom, however, the bottom will be barren of plant life.

That the euphotic zone does not extend to the bottom does not preclude an ecosystem from existing in it. Many species of phytoplankton—algae and photosynthetic bacteria that grow as single cells or in small groups of cells—can maintain themselves close to the surface in the euphotic zone. Phytoplankton may support a diverse food web, including many species of fish and sea mammals (such as whales).

Also, an entire ecosystem operates in the cold, dark depths below the euphotic layer nourished by detritus precipitation from above, and closer to the ocean floor, by vents and fissures that produce mineral-rich water and warmth.

In a phytoplankton-based system, nutrients dissolved in the water become critically important. If the water contains too few dissolved nutrients such as phosphorus or nitrogen compounds, the growth of phytoplankton and, hence, the rest of the ecosystem, will be limited. If the bottom receives light, it may support vegetation despite nutrient-poor water because such vegetation draws nutrients from the bottom materials. Indeed, nutrient-rich water may be counterproductive to bottom vegetation, because the dissolved nutrients support the growth of phytoplankton, which makes the water turbid and shades out the bottom vegetation.

Let us put these concepts together to understand particular marine environments. The most productive areas of the ocean—the areas supporting the most abundant marine life of all sorts—are mostly found within 200 miles (300 km) of shorelines. This is true because either the bottom is within the euphotic zone and thus supports abundant bottom vegetation, or nutrients washing in from the land support an abundant primary production of phytoplankton.

In the open ocean, there is less and less marine life as one moves farther from shore. Indeed, marine biologists speak of most of the open ocean as being a "biological desert." The lack of life occurs both because the bottom is well below the euphotic zone and because the water is nutrient poor.

The nutrients carried to the bottom with the settling detritus are released into solution by decomposers, thus making the bottom water nutrient rich. This nutrient-rich bottom water may be carried along by ocean currents. Where the currents hit underwater mountains or continental rims, the nutrient-rich water is brought to the surface. Phytoplankton flourish in these areas of **upwelling** (rising) nutrient-rich water and support a rich diversity of fish and marine mammals.

In sum, the world's oceans are far from uniformly stocked with fish. By far the richest marine fishing areas are continental shelves and regions of upwelling as shown on the accompanying map. Unfortunately, however, many of these areas are now being depleted by overfishing.

(Image is courtesy of Jane A. Elrod and Gene Feldman. NASA/Goddard Space Flight Center.)

Magenta—mid oceans: lowest productivity ( 0.1 mg chlorophyll/m³ or less).
Red/orange—along coasts: highest productivity (10 mg chlorophyll/m³ or more).

these compounds is achieved by growing the particular organism on suitable organic matter in a vessel without oxygen. In nature, **anaerobic**, or *oxygen-free*, environments commonly exist in the sediment at the bottom of marshes or swamps, buried deep in the earth, and in the guts of animals where oxygen does not penetrate readily. Methane gas is commonly produced in such locations. A number of large grazing animals, including cattle, maintain fermenting bacteria in their digestive systems in a mutualistic, symbiotic relationship similar to that just described for termites. Both cattle and termites produce methane as a result.

For simplicity, our orientation in this chapter is directed toward terrestrial ecosystems. It is important to realize that exactly the same processes occur in aquatic ecosystems. As aquatic plants and algae absorb dissolved carbon dioxide and mineral nutrients from the water, their photosynthetic production becomes the food and dissolved oxygen that sustain consumers and other heterotrophs. Likewise, aquatic heterotrophs return carbon dioxide and mineral nutrients to the aquatic environment. Of course, aquatic and terrestrial systems are never entirely isolated from one another, and exchanges between them go on all the time.

# Principles of Ecosystem Function

The preceding examination of how ecosystems function reveals that three common denominators underlie them all: (a) recycling of nutrients, (b) using sunlight as a basic energy source, and (c) populations are such that overgrazing does not occur. In turn, these common features reveal basic principles underlying the sustainability of ecosystems. Let us examine this further.

## Nutrient Cycling

Looking at the various inputs and outputs of producers, consumers, detritus feeders, and decomposers, you should be impressed by how they fit together. The products and byproducts of each group are the food and/or essential nutrients for the other. Specifically, the organic material and oxygen produced by green plants are the food and oxygen required by consumers and other heterotrophs. In turn, the carbon dioxide and other wastes generated when heterotrophs break down their food are exactly the nutrients needed by green plants. Such recycling is fundamental, for two reasons: (a) It prevents wastes, which would cause problems, from accumulating. (b) It assures that the ecosystem will not run out of essential elements. Thus, we uncover the **first basic principle of ecosystem sustainability:**

For sustainability, ecosystems dispose of wastes and replenish nutrients by recycling all elements.

If we reconsider the natural law of conservation of matter which says that atoms cannot be created, destroyed, nor changed, we can see that recycling is the only possible way to maintain a dynamic system, and the biosphere has mastered this to a profound degree. We can see this even more clearly by focusing on the pathways of three key elements: carbon, phosphorus, and nitrogen. Because these pathways all lead in circles, they are known as the *carbon cycle*, the *phosphorus cycle*, and the *nitrogen cycle*. (Note that energy is not recycled; it must be renewably supplied by sunlight.)

**The Carbon Cycle.** For descriptive purposes, it is convenient to start the carbon cycle (Fig. 3-14) with the "reservoir" of carbon dioxide molecules present in the air and dissolved in water. Through photosynthesis and further metabolism, carbon atoms from carbon dioxide become the carbon atoms of all the organic molecules making up the plant's body. Through food chains, the carbon atoms then move into and become part of the tissues of all the other organisms in the ecosystem. However, it is unlikely that a particular carbon atom will be passed through many organisms in any one cycle, because at each step there is a considerable chance that the consumer will break down the organic molecule in cell respiration. As this occurs, the carbon atoms are released back to the environment in molecules of carbon dioxide, which completes one cycle, but, of course, starts another. Likewise, burning organic material returns the carbon atoms locked up in the material to the air in carbon dioxide molecules.

No two successive cycles of a particular carbon atom are likely to be the same. Nor are the two cycles likely to be within the same ecosystem, because carbon in the atmosphere will be carried around the globe by wind. By calculating the total amount of carbon dioxide in the atmosphere and the amount of primary production (photosynthesis) occurring in the biosphere, scientists have concluded that about a third of the total atmospheric carbon dioxide is taken up in photosynthesis in a year, but an equal amount is returned to the atmosphere through cell respiration. This means that, on the average, a carbon atom makes a cycle from the atmosphere through one or more living things and back to the atmosphere every three years. What does this mean in terms of sharing earth's supply of carbon atoms with every other living thing that exists (or has existed) on Planet Earth? This fact is not without ethical implications. (See Ethics box, "Who Are You?" on page 73.)

**The Phosphorus Cycle.** The phosphorus cycle is representative of the cycles for all the mineral nutrients—

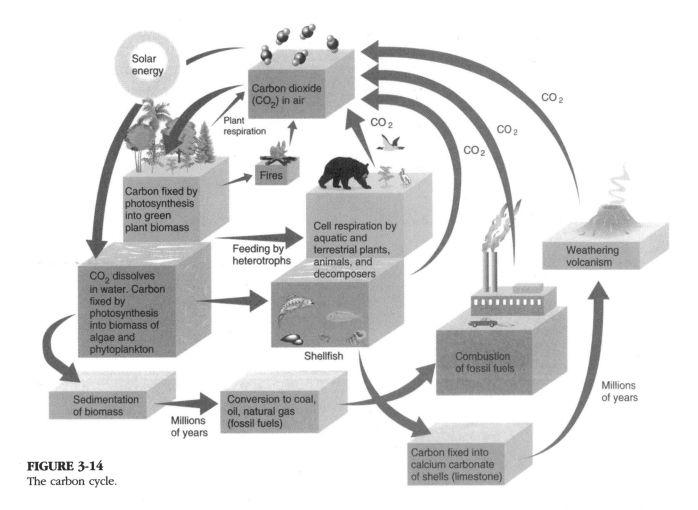

**FIGURE 3-14**
The carbon cycle.

those required elements that have their origin in rock and soil minerals (see Table 3-1). We focus on phosphorus for both simplicity and because its shortage tends to be a limiting factor in a number of ecosytems.

The phosphorus cycle is illustrated in Fig. 3-15. Phosphorus exists in various rock and soil minerals as the inorganic ion *phosphate* ($PO_4^{3-}$). As rock gradually breaks down, phosphate and other ions are released. Phosphate dissolves in water, but does not enter the air. Plants absorb phosphate from the soil or from a water solution, and when it is bonded into organic compounds by the plant, it is referred to as **organic phosphate**. Moving through food chains, organic phosphate is transferred from producers to the rest of the ecosystem. As with carbon, at each step there is a high likelihood that the organic compounds containing phosphate will be broken down in cell respiration, releasing inorganic phosphate in urine or other waste. The phosphate may then be reabsorbed by plants to start another cycle.

There is an important difference between the carbon cycle and the phosphorus cycle. No matter where carbon dioxide is released, it will mix into and

maintain the concentration of carbon dioxide in the air. Phosphate, however, which does not have a gas phase, is recycled only if the wastes containing it are deposited on the soil *from which it came*. The same holds true for other mineral nutrients. Of course, in natural ecosystems wastes (urine, detritus) are deposited in the same area so that recycling occurs efficiently. Humans have been extremely prone to interrupt this cycle, however.

A very serious case of humans disrupting the phosphorus cycle is the cutting of tropical rain forests. This type of ecosystem is supported by a virtually 100-percent-efficient recycling of nutrients. There are little or no reserves of nutrients in the soil. When the forest is cut and burned, the nutrients that were stored in the organisms and detritus are readily washed away by the heavy rains, and the land is thus rendered unproductive. Another human effect on the cycle is that much phosphate from agricultural crop lands makes its way into waterways—either directly, in runoff from the crop lands, or indirectly, in sewage effluents. Because there is essentially no return of phosphate from water to soil, this addition results in overfertilization of bodies of water, which in turn leads to a severe pollution problem

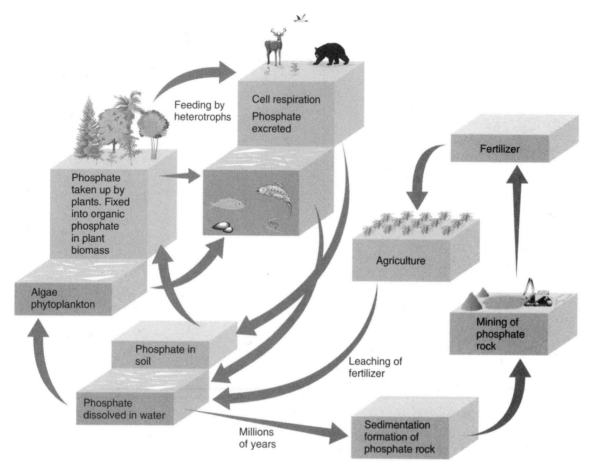

**FIGURE 3-15**
The phosphorus cycle.

known as eutrophication. (See Chapter 12.) Meanwhile, the lost phosphorus must be replaced on the crop lands by mining phosphate rock—a process that will ultimately result in depletion of the phosphate.

When humans use manure, compost (rotted plant wastes), or sewage sludge (see Chapter 13) on crops, lawns, or gardens, the foregoing natural cycle is duplicated. But in too many cases it is not, and the applied chemical fertilizers end up being leached (carried by water seepage) into waterways, resulting in eutrophication.

**The Nitrogen Cycle.** The nitrogen cycle (Fig. 3-16) is unique; it has aspects of both the carbon cycle and the phosphorus cycle. The main reservoir of nitrogen is the air, which is about 78% nitrogen gas ($N_2$). Plants and animals cannot utilize nitrogen gas directly from the air. Instead, the nitrogen must be in mineral form, such as ammonium ions ($NH_4^+$) or nitrate ions ($NO_3^-$). A number of bacteria and cyanobacteria (bacteria that contain chlorophyll; formerly referred to as blue-green algae) can convert nitrogen gas to the ammonium form, a process called biological **nitrogen fixation**. For terres-

trial ecosystems, the most important among these nitrogen-fixing organisms is a bacterium called *Rhizobium*, which lives in nodules on the roots of legumes, the plant family that includes peas and beans (Fig. 3-17). This is another example of mutualistic symbiosis: The legume provides the bacteria with a place to live and with food (sugar), and gains a source of nitrogen in return.

From the legumes, nitrogen is passed down whatever food chains exist. At each step, as we have observed before, the nitrogen-containing compounds may be broken down in cell respiration. As this occurs, nitrogen-compounds are returned to the soil with excrements and may be absorbed by other plants. Thus, after it is fixed, nitrogen may be recycled in a manner similar to phosphorus and other mineral nutrients. However, nitrogen does not remain in this "mineral phase" of the cycle indefinitely. Other kinds of bacteria in the soil gradually change the nitrogen compounds back to nitrogen gas (See Fig. 3-16). Consequently, nitrogen will not accumulate in the soil. Additionally, some nitrogen gas may enter the cycle by being converted to the ammonium form by discharges of light-

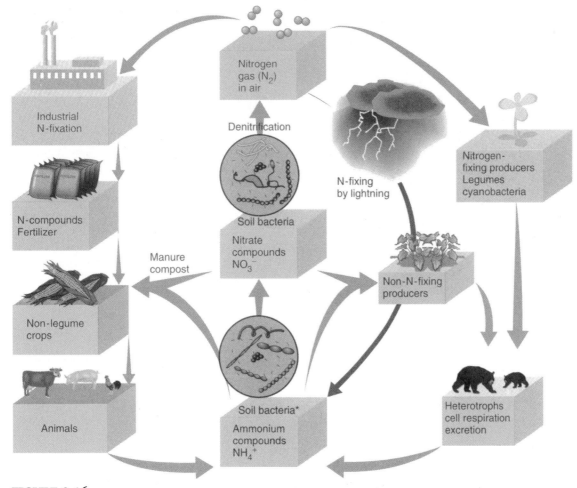

**FIGURE 3-16**
The nitrogen cycle.

ning in a process known as *atmospheric nitrogen fixation* and by coming down with rainfall. This pathway is estimated to be only about 10 percent of the biological pathway.

All natural ecosystems, then, depend on nitrogen-fixing organisms; legumes, with their symbiotic bacteria are, by far, the most important. The legume family includes a huge diversity of plants, ranging from clovers (common in grasslands) through desert shrubs to many trees. Every major terrestrial ecosystem, from tropical rain forest to desert and tundra, has its representative legume species, and legumes are generally the first plants to recolonize a burned-over area. Without them, all production would be sharply impaired because of lack of available nitrogen—precluding the formation of proteins, nucleic acids, and other building blocks of life.

The nitrogen cycle in aquatic ecosystems is similar. There, cyanobacteria are the most significant nitrogen fixers.

Only humans have been able to bypass the necessity for legumes when growing nonlegume crops such as corn, wheat, and other grains. We do this by fixing nitro-

gen in chemical factories (industrial nitrogen fixing). Synthetically produced ammonium and nitrate compounds are major constituents of fertilizer. However, the intensive use of such chemical fertilizer is not without disadvantages as regards maintaining a productive soil structure. Therefore, some farmers are readopting the natural process of enriching the soil by alternating legumes with nonlegume crops—that is, by **crop rotation**. This topic will be discussed further in Chapter 9.

While we have focused on the cycles of carbon, phosphorus, and nitrogen, it should be evident that cycles exist for oxygen, hydrogen, and all the other elements that play a role in living things. Also, while the routes taken by distinct elements may differ, it should be evident that all are going on simultaneously and that all come together in the tissues of living things.

From studying these cycles it might appear that every element is always recycled 100 percent. In fact there are some significant losses, or sinks, in the cycles. For example, carbon dioxide is removed from the cycle we have discussed by clams, oysters, and other marine organisms that use it in making their shells, which are

**FIGURE 3-17**
Nitrogen fixation. Conversion of nitrogen gas in the atmosphere to forms that can be used by plants, is carried out by bacteria that live in the root nodules of legumes. This process allows nitrogen gas to be converted into compounds needed for life. (USDA.)

calcium carbonate ($Ca_2CO_3$). Deposits of this calcium carbonate later convert to limestone, and thus the carbon atoms may remain trapped for hundreds of millions of years. Additionally, huge amounts of carbon were sidetracked millions of years ago in the formation of what are now our fossil fuels (see Chapter 21).

In the meantime, however, there is venting of carbon dioxide, as well as other gases, from volcanoes. On the millions-of-years time scale sea beds may be uplifted and carbon dioxide released from limestone by acidic leaching. Therefore, the cycles we have discussed are tied to much longer-term geological cycles; but over the millennia equilibrium is maintained. Will humans upset this equilibrium by burning the fossil fuels releasing the carbon dioxide over a relatively short period of time?

## Running on Solar Energy

We have seen that no system can run without an input of energy, and living systems are no exception. For all major ecosystems, both terrestrial and aquatic, the initial source of energy is *sunlight* absorbed by green plants through the process of photosynthesis. (The only exceptions are ecosystems near the ocean floor or in dark caves, where the producers are bacteria that derive energy from the oxidation of hydrogen sulfide in those locations. These bacteria use that energy to make

organic compounds, in a manner similar to that of higher plants. The process is called *chemosynthesis,* because it runs on chemical energy rather than light.)

Using sunlight as the basic energy source is fundamental to sustainability for two reasons: it is both *nonpolluting* and *nondepletable.*

*Nonpolluting.* Light from the Sun is a form of pure energy; it contains no substance that can pollute the environment. All the matter and pollution involved in the production of light energy are conveniently left behind on the Sun some 93 million miles (150 million kilometers) away in space.

*Nondepletable.* The Sun's energy output is constant. How much or how little of this energy is used on Earth will not influence, much less deplete, the Sun's output. For all practical purposes, the sun is an everlasting source of energy. True, astronomers tell us that the Sun will burn out in another 3–5 billion years, but we need to put this figure in perspective. One thousand is only 0.0001 percent of a billion. Thus, even the passing of millennia is hardly noticeable on this time scale.

Hence, we uncover the **second basic principle of ecosystem sustainability**:

> For sustainability, ecosystems use sunlight as their source of energy.

From the preceding discussion, you should be impressed with the importance of chemical nutrients and light as major prerequisites for the functioning of every ecosystem. Yet, we observed in Chapter 2 that rainfall and temperature (climate) are the primary limiting factors determining different terrestrial biomes. Basically, this is because every region that is above water receives abundant light, and most soils contain a modicum of nutrients or retain their nutrients through recycling. Therefore, light and nutrients are generally not limiting factors on land. But the situation is different in aquatic and marine environments, where light and nutrients dominate as the determining factors. (See the Global Perspective box, page 65.)

## Prevention of Overgrazing

We now return to the concept of the food or biomass pyramid presented in Chapter 2 (Fig. 2-14). We have seen that a consumer cannot gain an amount of weight equal to what it eats because first, 60–90 percent of what is consumed is broken down for energy and second, another portion passes through without being digested. These two facts by themselves would result in the declining biomass at each higher trophic level—the biomass pyramid observed. However, there is a third reason for the observed decline. It is the following.

In a grazing situation it is readily apparent that if

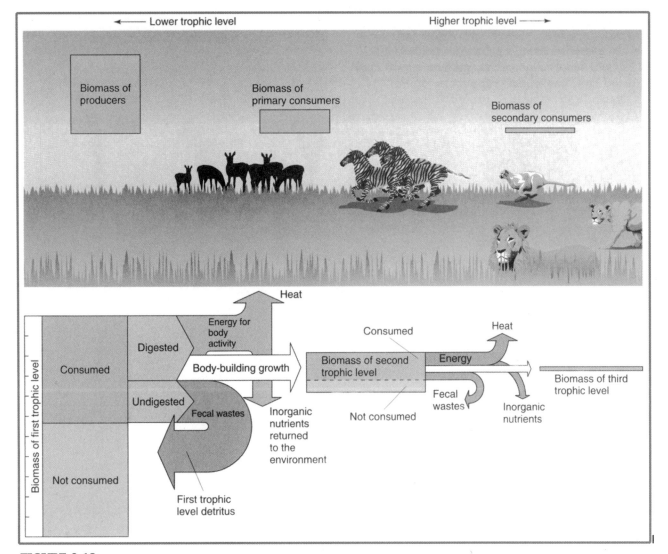

**FIGURE 3-18**
Decreasing biomass at higher trophic levels. The decrease results from three facts: (1) Much of the preceding trophic level is standing biomass and so is not available for consumption; (2) much of what is consumed is broken down in order to release energy; and (3) some of what is consumed passes through the organism.

the animals eat the grass faster than the grass can regrow, sooner or later the grass will be destroyed, and all the animals will starve. This situation is known as **overgrazing**. The same holds true in the case of carnivores and their prey. Basically, a sustainable situation demands that, on average, consumption cannot exceed production. It follows, then, that a large portion of the producer must remain intact to maintain that production. This portion, or population, that is not consumed, and which must remain intact to assure continued production, is called the **standing biomass**. In natural ecosystems, which are sustainable, we observe that consumers eat no more than a small proportion of the total biomass available; most is left as standing biomass (Fig. 3-18). We can readily see that this is another feature that is fundamental to sustainability. Hence, here is the **third basic principle of ecosystem sustainability**:

> For sustainability, the size of consumer populations is maintained so that overgrazing or other overuse does not occur.

How populations are regulated in nature to prevent such overuse will be the subject of Chapter 4. For now,

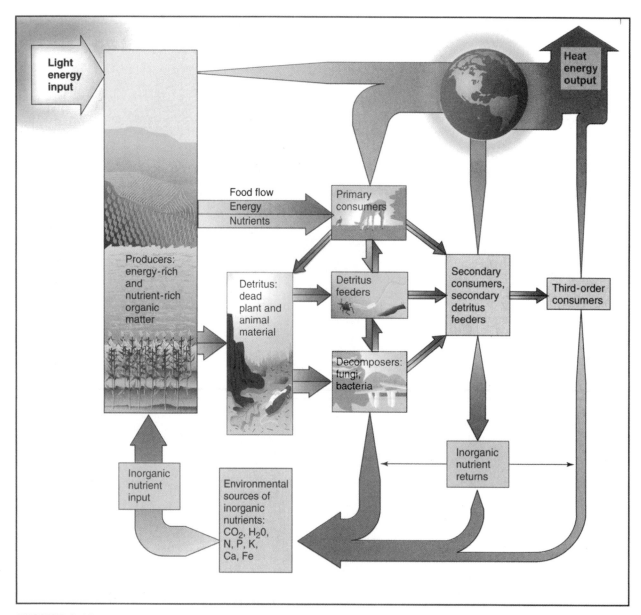

**Light energy input**

**Food flow**
**Energy**
**Nutrients**

Primary consumers

**Heat energy output**

Producers: energy-rich and nutrient-rich organic matter

Detritus: dead plant and animal material

Detritus feeders

Decomposers: fungi, bacteria

Secondary consumers, secondary detritus feeders

Third-order consumers

Inorganic nutrient returns

Inorganic nutrient input

Environmental sources of inorganic nutrients: $CO_2$, $H_2O$, N, P, K, Ca, Fe

**FIGURE 3-19**
Nutrient cycling in and energy flowing through an ecosystem. Arranging organisms by feeding relationships and depicting the energy and nutrient inputs and outputs of each relationship show a continuous recycling of nutrients (blue) in the ecosystem, a continuous flow of energy through it (red), and a decrease in biomass.

it is sufficient to appreciate that such regulation is mandatory for sustainability. The three basic principles of ecosystem sustainability are illustrated in Figure 3-19.

Recognizing these principles of ecosystem sustainability, many students attempt to make their own artificial ecosystems in sealed bottles, with varying degrees of success. One artificial ecosystem big enough to maintain people, Biosphere 2, has been built in Arizona. ("Earth Watch" box, Biosphere 2, page 75).

## Implications for Humans

We have said that a major part of our purpose in studying natural ecosystems lies in the fact that they are models of sustainability. We have said that if we can elucidate the principles that underlie their sustainability, we may be able to apply those principles toward our own efforts to achieve a sustainable society. Impor-

# Who Are You?

The cycling of carbon and other elements from the environment through organisms and back to the environment is more than just theory. Atoms can be made radioactive (see Appendix C) so that they behave chemically exactly like normal atoms, except that they give off radiation, which can be detected with suitable monitors. Introducing radioactive compounds into a cycle is analogous to planting a small radio transmitter on a vehicle to monitor where the vehicle goes. By this technique, scientists have verified that carbon atoms move from carbon dioxide in the atmosphere into glucose and then into various macromolecules making up plant tissues. Similarly, scientists can observe the progress of the radioactive atoms down food chains and their return to the atmosphere via cell respiration.

Through these studies, a striking fact becomes evident: All tissues of animal bodies, including our own, "turn over" quite rapidly. That is, although we maintain our general appearance from year to year, every tissue in our body is constantly being broken down, oxidized, and replaced with newly made molecules derived from the food we eat. Atom for atom, molecule for molecule, our bodies are entirely replaced about every four years. Thus, all forms of life, including human, are constantly participating in the cycles of all the elements.

Imagine having a microscope powerful enough to see the individual carbon atoms in the protein of the skin on your hand. Focus on a single carbon atom. Where did it come from? From the food you ate a few weeks ago? Before that? From carbon dioxide in the atmosphere that was incorporated into a plant by photosynthesis? Where will it go? In a few weeks, it will in all likelihood be back in the atmosphere as carbon dioxide after the top layer of your skin is sloughed off and oxidized by microorganisms. Will this be the end of the carbon atom's travels? No, it will no doubt go on to additional cycles.

If this or any other atom in your body could tell you its "life history," the story might go something like this:

I have existed since the formation of Earth. In my countless cycles from the air through living things and back, I have participated in the bodies of virtually every species that has ever existed anywhere on Earth, including trees and animals of the forests; seaweeds, fishes, and other creatures of the oceans; and the dinosaurs that roamed the land 100 million years ago. In more recent times, my travels along food chains have led through humans of all races, as well as other plants and animals that share your environment. This is my fate till the end of time.

In a very real and verifiable way, all life is interconnected through sharing and recycling a common pool of atoms. Generations pass, but atoms remain the same. Does the scientific fact that we are all continually sharing the same atoms with every human and other living creature on Earth have ethical and moral implications?

---

tantly, discovering and applying principles is different from simple copying. For example, birds were models for the ability to fly. However, human flight was not achieved by copying birds; indeed, such efforts failed. Flight was attained by studying birds and discovering principles of aerodynamic lift and guidance. By applying these principles to "human-built machines," we not only achieved flight, but surpassed the capability of birds manyfold.

The reverse holds true also. Forging ahead in a way that is out of keeping with basic principles, whether from ignorance, arrogance, or stupidity, assuredly leads to problems and perhaps much worse. Any number of disasters have resulted from people's failure to give adequate attention to principles of engineering, physics, chemistry, and so on.

We have discussed three of four specific principles regarding sustainability of living systems. (The fourth will be covered in Chapter 4.) Can we see our environmental problems in terms of failing to abide by these principles? Even more, can we see these principles as providing guideposts for achieving sustainable development? The following is a synopsis contrasting our human system with these first three principles of sustainability.

***First Principle of Sustainability.*** *For sustainability, ecosystems dispose of wastes and replenish nutrients by recycling all elements.*

In contrast to the remarkable recycling seen in natural ecosystems, we have constructed our human system, in large part, on the basis of a *one-directional flow* of elements. We have already noted that the fertilizer-nutrient phosphate, which is mined from deposits, ends up going into waterways with effluents from sewage treatment. The same one-way-flow can be seen in such metals as aluminum, mercury, lead, and

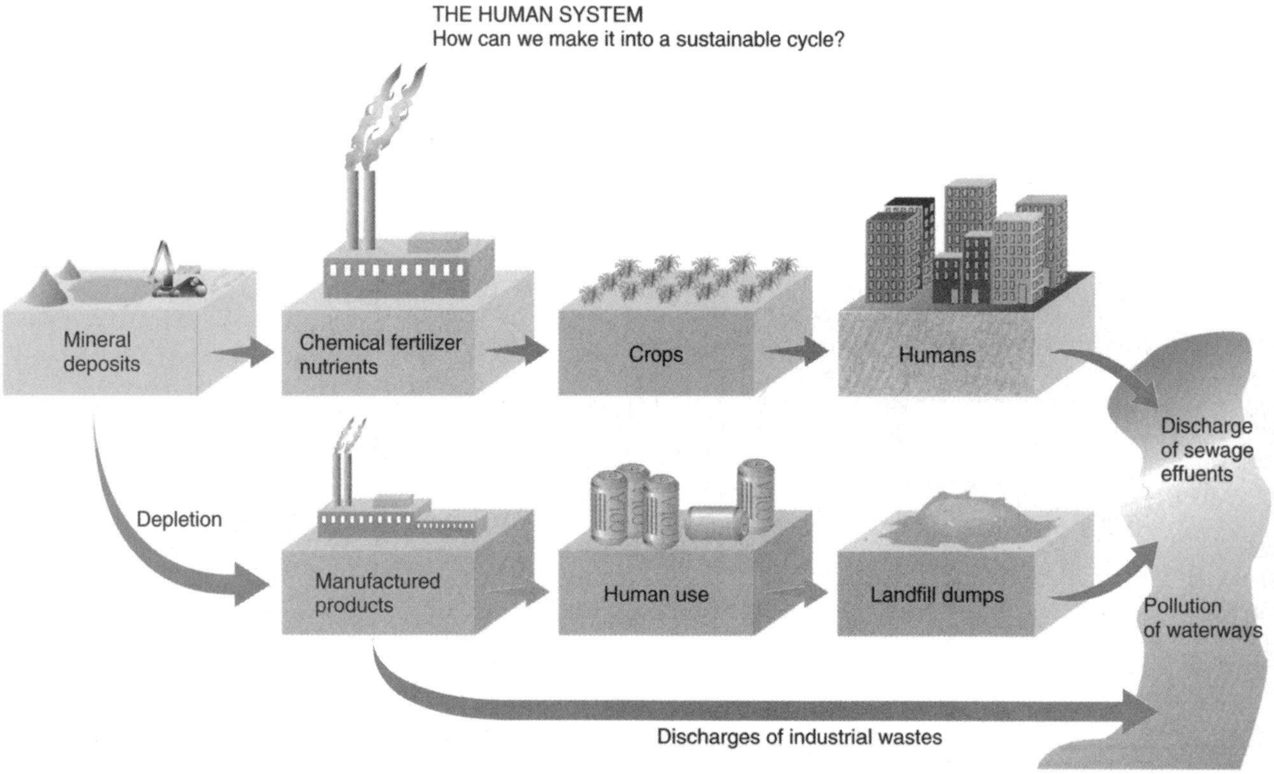

Mineral deposits → Chemical fertilizer nutrients → Crops → Humans

Depletion

Manufactured products → Human use → Landfill dumps

Discharge of sewage effluents

Pollution of waterways

Discharges of industrial wastes

**FIGURE 3-20**

In contrast to applying the ecological principle of nutrient recycling, human society has developed a pattern of one-directional nutrient flow. There are increasing problems at both ends. This drawing illustrates one-way flow for phosphorus, but the scheme also applies to all other elements we use in our daily lives.

cadmium, which are the "nutrients" of our industry. At one end, they are mined from the earth; at the other, they end up in dumps and landfills, as items containing them are discarded. Is it any wonder that there are depletion problems at one end and pollution problems at the other (Fig. 3-20)? Actually, pollution problems are most significant at the present time. The earth has vast deposits of most minerals, but the capacity of ecosystems (even the whole biosphere) to absorb wastes without being disturbed is comparatively limited. This limitation is aggravated even more by the fact that many of the products we use are nonbiodegradable. Conversely, can you see the rationale for expanding the concept of recycling to include, not just paper, bottles, and cans, but everything from sewage to industrial wastes as well?

***Second Principle of Sustainability.*** *For sustainability, ecosystems use sunlight as their source of energy.*

In contrast to running on solar energy, which is nonpolluting and nondepletable, we have constructed a human system that is heavily dependent on fossil fuels—coal, natural gas, and crude oil. Crude oil is the base for refinement of all liquid fuels: gasoline, diesel fuel, fuel oil, and so on. Even in the production of food,

which is fundamentally supported by sunlight and photosynthesis, it is estimated that we use about 10 calories of fossil fuel for every calorie of food consumed. This additional energy is used in the course of field preparation, fertilizing, controlling pests, harvesting, processing, preserving, transportation, and finally cooking.

Again, the most pressing problem in connection with consuming these fuels is the limited capacity of the biosphere to absorb the waste byproducts produced from burning them. Air pollution problems, including urban smog, acid rain, and the potential for global warming, are the result of these byproducts. Also problems stemming from depletion, particularly that of crude oil, are on the horizon. You see why most people concerned about sustainability are also solar-energy advocates. Solar energy is extremely abundant (Fig. 3-21). Just as important, we do have the technology to obtain most, if not all, of our energy needs from sunlight and the forces it causes such as wind (Fig. 3-22; see also Chapter 23).

***Third Principle of Sustainability.*** *For sustainability, the sizes of consumer populations are maintained so that overgrazing or other overuse does not occur.*

We have seen that, in natural ecosystems, a suit-

The proof of a theory lies in testing it. If the biosphere functions as we have described—running on solar energy and recycling all the elements from the environment through living organisms and back to the environment—then it should be possible to create an artificial biosphere that functions similarly. Indeed, students commonly conduct an exercise of creating a "biosphere in a bottle": Some photosynthetic and compatible consumer organisms are sealed in a bottle and kept in the light. Varying degrees of success are achieved, however; such systems usually do not sustain themselves beyond a few weeks for various reasons.

The largest such experiment to date is Biosphere 2, constructed in Arizona 30 miles north of Tucson. Biosphere 2 was developed entirely with private venture capital, with a view toward gaining information and experience that might be used in creating permanent space stations on the Moon or other planets or for long-distance space travel. Additionally, Biosphere 2 is expected to yield information that will further our understanding of our own biosphere—Biosphere 1.

Biosphere 2 is a supersealed "greenhouse," including seals underneath, enclosing an area of 2.5 acres (1 ha). Entry and exit is through a double air lock. Different environmental conditions within the containment support several ecosystems. Accordingly, there is an area of tropical rain forest, savannah, scrub forest, desert, fresh- and saltwater marshes, and a miniocean complete with a coral reef, each stocked with respective species—over 4000 in all. There is an agricultural area and living quarters for a crew of up to ten "Biospherians."

Water vapor from evaporation and transpiration of plants is condensed to create high rainfall over the tropical rain forest. The water trickles back toward the marshes and the ocean through soil filters, providing a continuous supply of fresh water for both humans and ecosystems. Carbon

(Gonzalo Arcila/Decisions Investments Corp.)

dioxide from respiration is reabsorbed and oxygen is replenished through photosynthesis. Thus, these "natural ecosystems" provide the basic ecological stability for the atmosphere and hydrosphere of Biosphere 2. All wastes, including human and animal excrements, are treated, decomposed, and recycled to support the growth of plants.

Biosphere 2 is not self-sufficient as regards solar energy falling on the structure. Biosphere 2's energy demands for machinery are such that an additional (30) acres (12 ha) of solar collectors would be required. (Actually, external natural gas–driven generators are used.)

The first crew of four men and four women, a crew with a variety of skills and academic backgrounds, completed the first two-year mission in September 1993. In addition to monitoring and collecting data on the natural systems, their main occupation was intensive organic agriculture (no chemical pesticides) to produce plant foods both for themselves and for feeding a few goats and chickens, which produced eggs, milk, and a little meat. Some fish farming supplied additional protein. The living quarters include the comforts and conveniences of modern living, but all communication with the outside world was via electronics. Their environment with other plants and animals is totally sealed from that of the outside world. In such a closed system, the water soil, and nutrients they had when they began were the same when they finished, having cycled inumerable times within the system.

At the end of their two-year experiment sojourn, the "Biospherians" emerged somewhat thinner, but all in good health. The overall conclusion is that it worked: It is possible to build a biosphere, that includes humans, and have it function within tolerable limits.

Not everything went perfectly. At one point additional oxygen had to be introduced, because the amount of oxygen that was absorbed by decomposers in the rich organic soil was underestimated. Excessive carbon dioxide was absorbed through chemical reactions with exposed concrete surfaces. A considerable number of species that were introduced, especially insect pollinators, became extinct, necessitating pollinating many plants by hand.

Some writers have suggested that if we trash our own planet, we may end up living in Biosphere 2-like enclosures, although the costs for such escape from a polluted environment would be prohibitive. An important lesson from Biosphere 2 is an appreciation of the operational complexity of Biosphere 1. If we fail to maintain our natural biosphere, there will be no alternative for survival.

Many scientific experiments continue within the sealed structure under the supervision of Columbia University's Lamont–Doherty Earth Observatory.

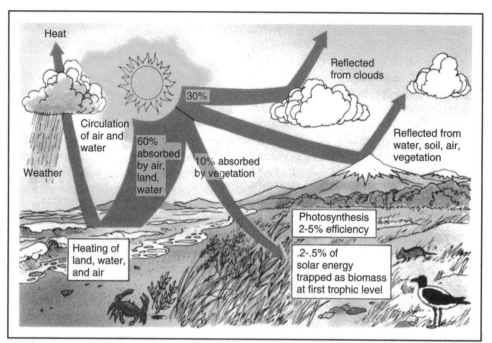

**FIGURE 3-21**
Of the total solar energy reaching Earth, 30% is reflected from clouds, water, and land surfaces. Sixty percent is absorbed by, and goes into heating land, water, and air. This heating causes evaporation of water and the circulation of air and water, resulting in weather. Only 10% of the solar energy is absorbed by vegetation. (Of course these percentages vary greatly among each ecosystem, the season of the year, and location on Earth.) Given the low efficiency of photosynthesis, only 2–5% of the 10% absorbed by vegetation (0.2–0.5% of the total solar energy) is trapped as biomass at the first trophic level, but this amount of energy supports all the rest of the ecosystem. It is estimated that just 0.1% of the solar energy arriving at Earth's surface would supply all human needs and not affect the dynamics of the biosphere.

able standing biomass is maintained so that future production is assured. Even a slight familiarity with such problems as the world's loss of biodiversity, loss of tropical rainforests, overfishing of the oceans, overgrazing of range lands, or other examples of overuse is enough to show that we are wanting with respect to this principle.

Nor are the causes of this overuse hard to identify—the demands of a rapidly growing human population and increasing per capita consumption. Human population has increased more than sixfold in the past 200 years, and it is continuing to increase at a rate of nearly 88 million people per year—10 times faster than in 1800 (Chapter 6). Can you see why the success or failure of efforts toward stabilizing population will have profound implications regarding sustainability?

The necessity of stabilizing population takes on even more importance when we consider another trend—increasing per capita consumption. Given the same basic human system, better lives translate into more consumption of virtually everything. A particular case in point is the human fondness for meat. A trend that par-

allels increasing affluence in every country observed is increasing meat consumption. Because of the principles involved in the biomass pyramid, it takes about 10 pounds of grain to grow a pound of meat [more for beef, less for chicken (Fig. 3-23)]. Therefore, for every increment of increase in meat consumption, there is a tenfold increase in the demand on plant production and on all the land use, fertilizer, pesticides, energy, and pollution that that increase entails. Of course, the reverse is also true. Dropping down a trophic level alleviates the demand proportionally. The implication of this is profound when you consider that half the cultivated acreage in the U.S. produces animal feed!

In this brief assessment of our human system in relation to the principles of sustainability, we see that we are missing the mark by a wide margin, and the environmental troubles we face can be seen as a mounting consequence. We can use an awareness of our present circumstance as a guide to show the directions to be taken to attain a sustainable future. Specific things we can do will become obvious as we discuss the issues in later chapters.

**FIGURE 3-22**
Wind turbines generating electrical power in Palm Springs, CA. More than 50,000 wind turbines have been installed worldwide since 1974—15,000 in California alone. By the middle of the next century, wind-generated electricity will be a necessity, along with other renewable energy sources, conservation, and energy efficiency. (Matt Meadows/Peter Arnold, Inc.)

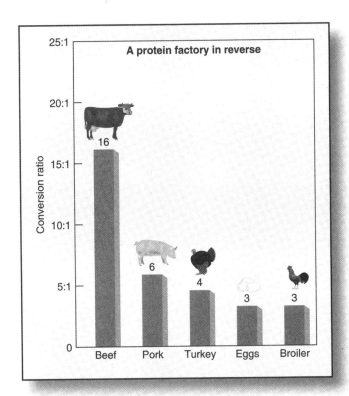

**FIGURE 3-23**
To obtain one pound of meat, poultry, or eggs, farmers must invest these many pounds of grains and soy feeds. To get one pound of beef requires an expenditure of 16 pounds of feed. Said another way, the grain consumed to support one person eating meat could support 16 persons eating the grains directly.

# ～ Review Questions

1. What are the six key elements of living organisms, and where does each occur in the environment? In four cases, identify the specific molecule that the element comes from.

2. Give a simple description of what is happening to the six key elements in the course of growth and decay. What is the "common denominator" that distinguishes organic and inorganic molecules?

3. State the definitions of matter and energy. Name three main categories of matter, and list four forms of kinetic energy.

4. Give five examples that demonstrate different conversions among forms of kinetic energy. Give another five examples that demonstrate conversions between kinetic and potential energy.

5. Name the two energy laws and apply each, describing the relative amounts and forms of energy going into and coming out of the conversions listed in Question 4.

6. What is chemical energy? What energy changes are involved in the formation and breakdown of organic molecules?

7. Describe the process of photosynthesis in terms of what is happening to specific atoms (matter) and where energy is coming from and going to. Do the same for cell respiration.

8. Food ingested by a consumer follows three different pathways. Describe each pathway in terms of what happens to the food involved and what products and byproducts are produced in each case.

9. Define and contrast starvation and malnutrition, giving the causes and results of each.

10. Compare and contrast the decomposers with other consumers in terms of matter and energy changes that they perform.

11. Where do carbon, phosphorus, and nitrogen exist in the environment, and how do they move into and through organisms and back to the environment?

12. In what forms does energy enter, move through, and leave ecosystems?

13. What three factors account for decreasing biomass at higher trophic levels—that is, the food pyramid?

14. What is meant by standing biomass? What does it imply regarding consumer populations?

15. What are the three principles of ecosystem sustainability?

16. Contrast our human system with each of the principles of sustainability. What environmental problems result from not abiding by the principles? What would you recommend regarding directions to achieve sustainability?

# ∼ *Thinking Environmentally*

1. Describe the consumption of fuel by a car in terms of the laws of conservation of matter and energy. That is, what are the inputs and outputs of matter and energy? (*Note*: Gasoline is an organic carbon-hydrogen compound.)

2. Relate your level of exercise, breathing hard, and "working up an appetite" to cell respiration in your body. What materials are consumed, and what products and byproducts are produced?

3. Using your knowledge of photosynthesis and cell respiration, create an illustration showing the hydrogen cycle and the oxygen cycle.

4. Write a short essay supporting or contradicting the statement, "Waste is a human concept and invention; it does not exist in natural ecosystems!"

5. Tundra and desert ecosystems support a much smaller biomass of animals than do tropical rainforests. Give two reasons for this fact.

6. Evaluate the sustainability of parts of the human system, such as transportation, manufacturing, agriculture, and waste disposal, by relating them to specific principles of sustainability. How can such things be modified to make them more sustainable?

7. In Chapter 2, we observed that humans have overcome the *usual* limits and barriers that restrict other species. Does this mean that we can disregard basic ecological principles? What is the difference between "usual limits" that restrict other species and the "basic principles" revealed here?

# APPENDIX 2

"The Diffusion of Languages," from *Human Geography: Culture, Society, and Space* by H.J. de Blij and Alexander B. Murphy. Copyright © 1999 John Wiley & Sons. This material used by permission of John Wiley & Sons, Inc.

Figure 9.1 reprinted with permission from T. V. Gamkrelidze and V. V. Ivanov, "The Early History of Indo-European Languages," *Scientific American*, March 1990, p. 111. Copyright © 1990 by Thomas Moore. All rights reserved.

Figure 9.2 reprinted with permission from T. V. Gamkrelidze and V. V. Ivanov, "The Early History of Indo-European Languages," *Scientific American*, March 1990, p. 112. Copyright © 1990 by Thomas Moore. All rights reserved.

Figure 9.4 reprinted with permission from Philip E. Ross, "Hard Words," *Scientific American*, April 1991, p. 139. Copyright © 1991 by Ian Worpole. All rights reserved.

Figure 9.5, by Johnny Johnson, reprinted with permission from "The Origins of Indo-Languages," by Colin Refrew. Copyright © October 1989 by Scientific American, Inc. All rights reserved.

Figure 9.6, by Johnny Johnson, reprinted with permission from "The Austonesian Dispersal and the Origin of Languages" by Peter Bellwood. Copyright © July 1991 by Scientific American, Inc. All rights reserved.

Figure 9.7 reprinted with permission from R. Lewin, "American Indian Language Dispute," *Science 242*, 1988, p. 1633. Copyright © 1988 American Association for the Advancement of Science.

# Chapter 9

# The Diffusion
# of Languages

## *From the field notes*

"Latin Spoken here . . . two thousand years ago. Travel the British country-side from Hampshire to Hadrian's Wall, and marvel at the impact the Romans made on their distant western outpost. Even here in the rugged Cumbrian Mountains facing the Irish Sea, where winters are severe and surface travel is difficult to this day, the Romans established a presence whose remnants still survive. But their linguistic legacy does not; what might have become another Romance-language-speaking area fell to the Anglo-Saxons. Today English, a member of the Germanic subfamily of languages, prevails here, and these ruins evince a linguistic diffusion that failed."

◆ The search for the origins of language goes back tens of thousands of years. It has yielded information not only about how language changes but also about the environments where early languages were spoken.

◆ Scientists do not yet agree on how long ago language emerged. Some believe that the use of language began with the rise of *Homo sapiens* 200,000 or more years ago; others argue that simple vocal communication began much earlier.

◆ Languages change through divergence, convergence, and replacement, making the spatial search for origins problematic.

◆ The Pacific and American realms, where languages spread relatively recently, provide useful information for the reconstruction of language-diffusion routes and processes.

◆ Writing, technology, and political organization play a key role in the diffusion of individual languages.

The world today is a Babel of languages, a patchwork of tongues. Nevertheless, it is possible to identify some languages that are related, such as Spanish and Portuguese, which are so similar that their common origin and recent divergence are beyond doubt. In fact, there is a historical record of this process. It reveals how the Latin of Roman times gave rise to the Romance languages of today (the major ones being Italian, Spanish, Portuguese, French, and Romanian). In just a few centuries Latin, which had been spoken in territories extending from Britain to the Bosporus, was replaced by a set of derivative languages.

Given the speed and thoroughness of this process, can we hope to unlock the mysteries of much earlier languages and retrace the evolution of modern languages from what linguists call the Mother Tongue, the first language spoken by *Homo sapiens sapiens* perhaps as long as 200,000 years ago? That remains an elusive goal, but with the help of computers, remarkable progress is being made in the reconstruction of ancient languages and their paths of diffusion. This chapter focuses on the relevance of linguistic theory and research to historical geography.

## ◆ TRACING LINGUISTIC DIVERSIFICATION

The diversification of languages has long been charted through the analysis of *sound shifts*. Take the Latin word for milk (*lacte*) and note that it becomes *latta* in Italian, *leche* in Spanish, and *lait* in French. Or the Latin for the number eight (*octo*), which becomes *otto*, *ocho*, and *huit*, respectively. Even if the Latin roots for

these words had never been known, linguists would have been able to deduce them.

This technique of backward reconstruction is crucial to linguistic research. If it is possible to deduce a large part of the vocabulary of an extinct language, it may be feasible to go even further and re-create the language that preceded it. This technique, called *deep reconstruction*, has yielded some important results. It takes humanity's linguistic family tree back thousands of years.

More than two centuries ago William Jones, an Englishman living in South Asia, undertook a study of Sanskrit, the language in which ancient Indian religious and literary texts were written. Jones discovered that the vocabulary and grammatical forms of Sanskrit bore a striking resemblance to the ancient Greek and Latin he had learned while in college. "No philologer [student of literature] could examine all three," Jones wrote, "without believing them to have sprung from some common source, which, perhaps, no longer exists." In the late eighteenth century this was a revolutionary notion indeed.

During the nineteenth century Jacob Grimm, a scholar as well as a writer of fairy tales, suggested that sound shifts might prove the relationships between languages in a scientific manner. He pointed out that related languages have similar, but not identical, consonants. (Consonants are formed by the constriction of the sound channel.) He believed that these consonants would change over time in a predictable way. Hard consonants, such as the **v** and **t** in the German word *vater*, would soften into va**d**er (Dutch) and **f**ather (English). Looking backward, we should expect to find the opposite: a hardening of consonants.

From Jones's notions and Grimm's ideas came the first major linguistic hypothesis, which proposed the existence of an ancestral *(Proto) Indo-European* language (or closely related languages), the predecessor of Latin, Greek, and Sanskrit, among other ancient languages. This concept had major implications because the proposed ancestral language(s) would link not only the present and past Romance language but also a number of other languages spoken from Britain to North Africa and South Asia.

Several research tasks followed from this hypothesis. First, the vocabulary of the proposed ancestral language must be reconstructed. Second, the hearth or source where this language originated, and from which it spread, must be located. Third, the routes of diffusion by which this dispersal took place should be traced. And fourth, researchers should attempt to learn about the ways of life of those who spoke this language.

## ◆ THE LANGUAGE TREE

Proto-Indo-European gave rise to more than Latin, Greek, and Sanskrit. As Figure 8-2 reminds us, the Indo-European language realm includes not only languages derived from Latin but also the Slavonic (Slavic) languages, including Russian, Ukrainian, Polish, Czech, Slovak, Bulgarian, and Slovenian, and the Germanic languages, including German, Swedish, Danish, and Norwegian. These, too, must have had common ancestors, branches of the Proto-Indo-European "tree."

### Divergence

The first scholar to compare the world's language families to the branches of a tree was August Schleicher, a German linguist. In the mid-nineteenth century he suggested that the basic process of language formation is *language divergence*, that is, differentiation over time and space. Languages would branch into dialects; isolation then increased the differences between dialects. Over time, dialects would become discrete languages, as happened with Spanish and Portuguese and is now happening with Quebecois French. Although this idea was later challenged, it stood the test of time, and the language-tree model remains central to language research (Fig. 9-1).

### Convergence

A complicating factor, however is human mobility. While languages diverged, people migrated as well. Languages did not merely diffuse through static populations; they were also spread by relocation diffusion

(see Chapter 2). Sometimes such diffusion caused long-isolated languages to make contact, creating **language convergence**. Such instances create special problems for researchers because the rules of reconstruction may not apply or may be unreliable.

### Replacement

A further complication should be considered in view of modern cultural events. We know that the languages of traditional, numerically smaller, and technologically less advanced peoples have been replaced, or greatly modified, by the languages of invaders. This process of **language replacement** goes on today, and there is every reason to believe that it has happened ever since humans began to use language. (In the next chapter we discuss the process of *creolization*, a form of language replacement now occurring in the Caribbean region and elsewhere.)

Reconstructing even a small branch of the language tree, therefore, is a complicated task. Look again at the language map of Europe (Fig. 8-3). If only *all* the languages were members of the same family, the same branch of the tree! But things are not that simple. Hungarian, completely surrounded by Indo-European languages, is not in the same family as any of its neighbors. Finnish is another non-Indo-European language, apparently distantly related to Hungarian but mapped as a member of a discrete subfamily. Estonian is more closely related to Finnish, as the map suggests. But a tantalizing enigma is presented by Basque, a family that is now isolated in a small region of northern Spain and southwestern France. What ancient proto-language gave rise to Basque? Similar questions arise in hundreds of places throughout the world, where linguistic islands survive despite later waves of language diffusion.

## ◆ THEORIES OF LANGUAGE DIFFUSION

While linguists reconstructed Proto-Indo-European vocabulary, human geographers and other scholars searched for the source of Proto-Indo-European. Identifying this hearth would enormously increase their understanding of Eurasian historical geography.

The linguists' research produced many valuable clues. Reconstructions by scholars working independently often produced remarkably similar results. The proto-language(s) had words for certain landforms, trees, and other features of the natural landscape, but it lacked others. Such information helps reveal the environment in which a language may have developed. For example, if a reconstructed language has no word for *snow*, this would suggest a tropical or equatorial

**INDO-EUROPEAN BRANCHES OF THE LANGUAGE TREE**

**Figure 9-1 Indo-European Branches of the Language Tree.** *Source: From T. V. Gamkrelidze and V. V. Ivanov, "The Early History of Indo-European Languages,"* Scientific American, *March 1990, p. 111.*

origin. If there is no word for *palm* tree, the language is likely to have emerged in a cold region. More specifically, if a certain type of vegetation (oak, pine, beech, birch, tall or short grass) is part of the vocabulary, the search for the environment where the language developed can be narrowed down—although researchers must factor in a time dimension, as environments have changed even during the Holocene. Time is less an issue when vocabulary refers to physiographic features of the landscape. If there are many words for mountains and hills but few for flat land, we can conclude that the source area was mountainous.

## Conquest Theory

Analyses of this kind produced a tentative answer to the geographic question. The Proto-Indo-European homeland source, it seemed, lay somewhere north of the Black Sea in the vast steppes of present-day Ukraine and Russia. The time, it was suggested, was more than 5000 years ago, and judging from the reconstructed vocabulary, the people used horses, had developed the wheel, and traded widely in many goods. The logical conclusion seemed to be that these early speakers of Proto-Indo-European spread westward on horseback, overpowering earlier inhabitants and beginning the diffusion and differentiation of Latin, Germanic, and Slavonic languages.

This *conquest theory* of language dispersal in Europe west of the Russian plains was long supported by a majority of archeologists, linguists, and human geographers. The sound shifts in the derivative languages (*vater* to *vader* to *father*, for example) seemed to represent a long period of westward divergence. The location of older Indo-European languages on western margins (Breton in France, Scottish Gaelic and Welsh in Britain, and Irish Gaelic in Ireland) appeared to be due to the arrival of newer languages from the east.

## Agriculture Theory

But not all scholars were convinced. As the archeological record in Europe became better known, other hypotheses were proposed. Luca Cavalli-Sforza and Robert Ammerman suggested that it was the spread of agriculture, not conquest, that diffused the Proto-Indo-European language through Europe. This, of course, meant that the source area of the ancient language would have had to lie in an area of agricultural innovation, not in the Ukrainian-Russian grasslands where pastoralism was the prevailing way of life. But where was this hearth? Was it in the Fertile Crescent of the Middle East? Apparently not, because the vocabulary of Proto-Indo-European has few words for plains but many terms for high and low mountains,

valleys, mountain streams, rapids, lakes, and other high-relief landforms.

In 1984 the Soviet scholars Thomas Gamkrelidze and Victor Ivanov, who reconstructed much of the known vocabulary of Proto-Indo-European, published a book in which they reported that these terms were supplemented by words for trees such as mountain oak, pine, fir, willow, and ash. The language also had names for animals such as lions, leopards, and monkeys—none of which lived in the plains north of the Black Sea. Thus arose the *agriculture theory* (as opposed to the conquest theory) and its proposed source area: the mountainous, well-watered terrain of Anatolia in modern Turkey. The archeological record indicates that there, between 7000 and 9000 years ago, the horse had been domesticated and the wheel was in use. The realm's leading hearth of agricultural innovation lay in nearby Mesopotamia.

**Support for the Theory** In 1991 the agriculture theory received support from analyses of the protein (that is, gene) content of individuals from several thousand locations across Europe. This research confirmed the presence of distance decay in the geographic pattern: certain genes became steadily less common from southern Turkey across the Balkans and into Western and northern Europe. This pattern was interpreted as showing that the farming peoples of Anatolia moved steadily westward and northward. As they did so, they mixed with nonfarming peoples, diluting their genetic identity as the distance from their source area increased. Archeologists Robert Sokal, Neal Olden, and Chester Wilson argued that farming led to an unprecedented increase in population and that this in turn stimulated migration. As a result, a slow but steady wave of farmers dispersed into Europe.

The agriculture theory can be used to explain a number of features of the language map of Europe. Ammerman and Cavalli-Sforza proposed that for every generation (25 years) the agricultural frontier moved approximately 18 kilometers (11 miles). This would mean that the European frontier would have been completely penetrated by farmers in about 1500 years, which is close to what the archeological record suggests. But some of the nonfarming societies in their path held out, and their languages did not change. Thus Etruscan did not become extinct until Roman times, and Basque survives to this day as a direct link to Europe's pre-farming era.

**Drawbacks of the Theory** The agriculture theory has some drawbacks, however. The Anatolian region is not an ideal environment for farming, and there is no strong archeological evidence for an agricultural culture hearth there. In addition, despite the genetic gradient identified in Europe, some language geographers

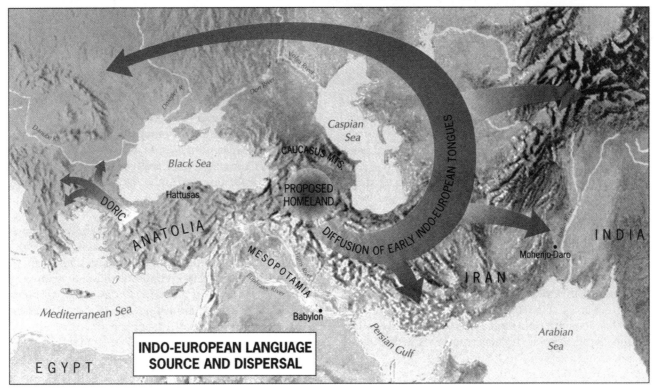

**Figure 9-2 Indo-European Language Source and Dispersal.** Postulated diffusion of an Indo-European proto-language. *Source: From T. V. Gamkrelidze and V. V. Ivanov,* Scientific American, *March 1990, p. 112.*

continued to prefer the dispersal hypothesis, which holds that the Indo-European languages that arose from the proto-language(s) were first carried eastward into Southwest Asia, then around the Caspian Sea, and then across the Russian-Ukrainian plains and on into the Balkans (Fig. 9-2). As is so often the case, there may be some truth in both hypotheses. If Anatolia was the source, the diffusion of Indo-European languages (that is, dialects of Proto-Indo-European) could have spread both westward across southern Europe *and* in the broad arc shown in Figure 9-3. In any case, an eastward diffusion must have occurred in view of the re-

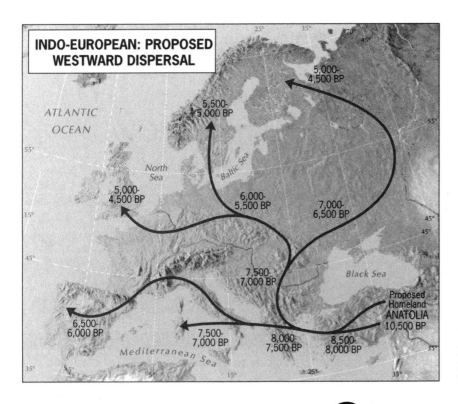

**Figure 9-3 Indo-European Proposed Westward Dispersal.** The approximate timing of the westward dispersal of the Indo-European languages.

lationships between Sanskrit and ancient Latin and Greek described by William Jones.

The geographic story of Proto-Indo-European is still unfolding, but this has not deterred researchers from going back even further. What was the ancestral language for Proto-Indo-European?

## ◆ THE SEARCH FOR A SUPERFAMILY

The evolution and diffusion of Proto-Indo-European occurred over a period of, at most, 9000 years. But language development and divergence have been going on for ten times as long or more; we have just dissected a thin branch of an old, gnarled tree (Fig. 9-4).

This does not discourage modern linguists or language geographers, however. The British scholar

Colin Renfrew carried the agriculture theory a step further by proposing that not just one but three agricultural hearths gave rise to language families (Fig. 9-5). From the Anatolian source diffused Europe's Indo-European languages; from the western arc of the Fertile Crescent came the languages of North Africa and Arabia; and from the Fertile Crescent's eastern arc ancient languages spread into present-day Iran, Afghanistan, Pakistan, and India, later to be replaced by Indo-European languages.

Russian scholars have long been in the forefront of research on ancient languages, but their work was not well known in the West until recently. The work of two scholars in particular has had great impact. Starting in the 1960s, Vladislav Illich-Svitych and Aharon Dolgopolsky tackled a daunting problem: deep reconstruction of the language that was ancestral to Proto-Indo-European. Using words that are assumed to be the most stable and dependable parts of

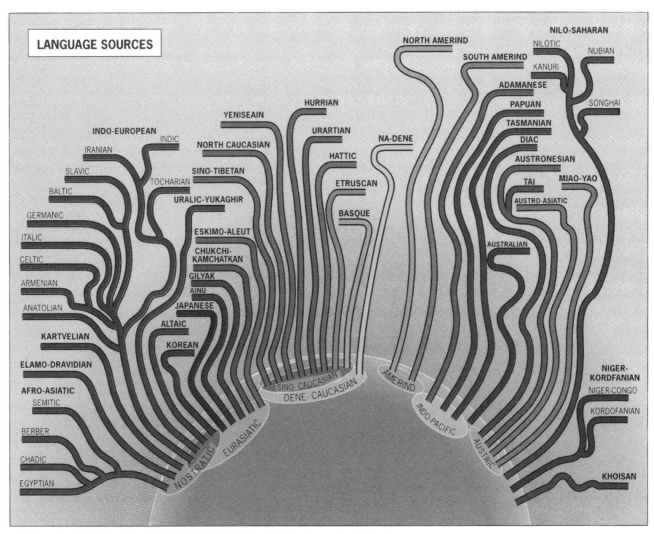

**Figure 9-4 Language Sources.** *Source: After a diagram in Philip E. Ross, "Hard Words," Scientific American, April 1991, p. 139.*

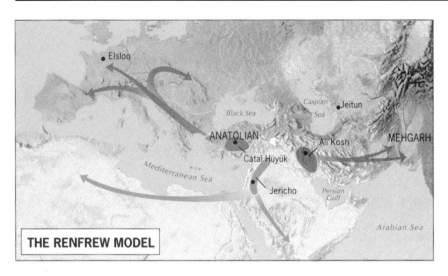

**Figure 9-5 The Renfrew Model.** The Renfrew Model poses that three source areas of agriculture each gave rise to a great language family. *Source: From "The Origins of Indo-European Languages,"* Scientific American, *1989, p. 114.*

a language's vocabulary (such as those identifying arms, legs, feet, hands, and other body parts, and terms for the sun, moon, and other elements of the natural environment), they reconstructed an inventory of several hundred words. What was most remarkable is that they did this independently, each unaware of the other's work for many years. When finally they met and compared their inventories, they found that they were amazingly similar. They agreed that they had established the core of a pre-Proto-Indo-European language, which they named **Nostratic**.

As with Proto-Indo-European, the evolving vocabulary of the Nostratic language revealed much about the lives and environments of its speakers. There apparently were no names for domesticated plants or animals, so Nostratic-speakers were hunter-gatherers, not farmers. An especially interesting conclusion had to do with the words for *dog* and *wolf*, which turned out to be the same, suggesting that the domestication of wolves may have been occurring at the time. The oldest known bones of dogs excavated at archeological sites date from about 14,000 years ago, so Nostratic may have been in use at about that time, well before the First Agricultural Revolution.

Nostratic is believed to be the ancestral language not only of Proto-Indo-European, and thus the Indo-European language family as a whole, but also of the Kartvelian languages of the southern Caucasus region (16 in Fig. 8-2), the Uralic-Altaic languages (which include Hungarian and Finnish, Turkish and Mongolian), the Dravidian languages of India (Fig. 8-5), and the Afro-Asiatic language family, in which Arabic is dominant.

How long *before* 14,000 years B.P. (Before the Present) it may have been in use has not yet been established. The same is true of Nostratic's geography. Where Nostratic was born, and what tongues gave rise to it, are unanswered questions. However, Nostratic links languages that are separated even more widely

than those of the Indo-European family today. Some scholars have suggested that Nostratic (and its contemporaries, variously named Eurasiatic, Indo-Pacific, Amerind, and Austric) is a direct successor of a proto-world language that goes back to the dawn of human history, but this notion is highly speculative. The inset in Figure 9-1 reminds us how little of the human language tree we know with any certainty.

## ◆ DIFFUSION TO THE PACIFIC AND THE AMERICAS

The final stages of the dispersal of the older languages—before the global diffusion of English and other Indo-European languages—occurred in the Pacific realm and in the Americas. One would assume that the historical geography of these events would be easier to reconstruct than the complex situation in western Eurasia. After all, the peoples who canoed across the Pacific brought their languages to unpopulated islands. Similarly, there was no linguistic convergence with preexisting languages in the Americas. Therefore, if we needed a testing ground for linguistic divergence without "noise," the Pacific islands and the Americas would seem to be fine natural laboratories. But when we examine the debates over Pacific and American native languages, we find that the problems involved are not simple at all.

### Pacific Diffusion

In our discussion of human dispersal, we noted how late people first arrived in the Pacific islands; Polynesians reached New Zealand little more than 1000 years ago. On the other hand, Australia was reached between 50,000 and 60,000 years ago, and New Guinea's first human population must have arrived even earlier because the route to the southern landmass passed

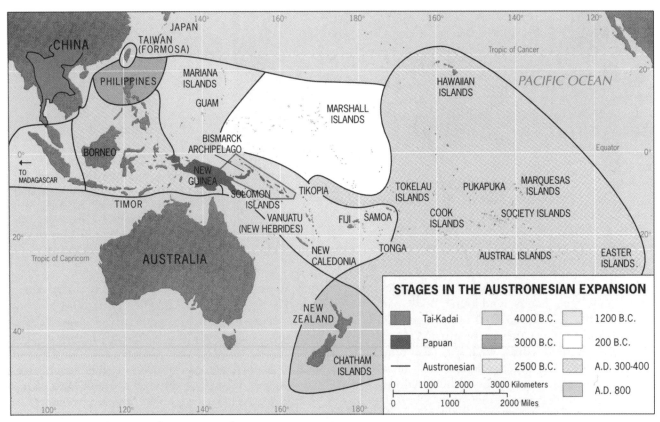

**Figure 9-6 Stages in the Austronesian Expansion.** Bellwood's Pacific-realm model shows the stages in the expansion of Austronesian languages. *Source: Adapted from P. Bellwood, "The Austronesian Dispersal and the Origin of Languages,"* Scientific American, *1991, p. 88.*

through it. Papuans as well as Native Australians were hunter-gatherers, although there is archeological evidence that root-crop cultivation began in New Guinea as long as 6000 years ago, leading to population growth and the expansion of Papuan populations eastward into the Solomon Islands and westward into present-day Indonesia. This expansion brought farmers into contact with foragers, and as a result the language mosaic of New Guinea and nearby islands is extremely complex.

But the diffusion of peoples and their languages into the Pacific north of Indonesia and New Guinea did not begin from these areas. Instead, it began in coastal China, where farming was well established. The languages of China and Southeast Asia had undergone several transitions; the sequence probably was similar to that from the pre-farmers' Nostratic to the farmers' Proto-Indo-European. An ancestral language gave rise to the Austro-Tai family of languages, and out of this family arose *Austronesian*. Language geographers believe that speakers of this language (with many words for rice, field, farm, water buffalo, plow, and canoe) reached Taiwan about 6000 years ago. Several centuries later, Austronesian speakers

managed to reach the Philippines. This movement resulted in the division of Austronesian into two dialects that later developed into major subfamilies. One of these, *Malayo-Polynesian*, became the forerunner of a large number of languages, including those spoken by the first settlers of Madagascar, the islands of Melanesia and Micronesia, Fiji (where *Fijian* was a discrete Malayo-Polynesian offshoot), and New Zealand, whose Maori people speak *Polynesian*, another derivative of this branch.

Considering the water-fragmented nature of the Pacific realm, this process of diffusion took place remarkably quickly. We may wonder why it took so long for the Agricultural Revolution in East Asia to stimulate emigration onto the islands off Asia's coast; but then the migrants rapidly spread from Madagascar in the west to Easter Island in the east. The whole eastern region of Polynesia was settled within several centuries (Fig. 9-6).

Although the lineages of Austronesian languages are better understood today, much remains to be learned about the reasons behind the complexity of the Pacific language map. Did successive waves of invasion stimulate divergence among the Malayo-

Polynesian languages? Or was differentiation due to isolation? And there remains the question of Austronesian ancestries. Linguists do not have a model similar to Nostratic for the languages of the Asian mainland. The Pacific language arena thus is anything but simple.

## Diffusion in the Americas

As Figure 8-2 indicates, the current language map of the Americas is dominated by Indo-European languages. These have engulfed the languages spoken in America for thousands of years—the languages of Native Americans.

The Native American population never was very large by modern standards. Estimates of its pre-Columbian population have increased over the years as anthropologists have learned more about these peoples, but even the highest estimate puts the number of Native Americans at 40 million just before the European invasion. As noted previously, it was long believed that the Native Americans arrived via the Bering land bridge from Asia and that the earliest immigrations occurred just 12,000 to 13,000 years ago. Given the modest numbers of people involved and their recent arrival, one would assume under this scenario that the linguistic situation should be fairly simple. There were no preexisting peoples to be absorbed and no lifeways to be transformed. At the very least, the pattern should be much simpler than that of Eurasia.

These conclusions may be wrong, however. While some 40 language families have been recognized in the Old World, linguists have identified as many as 200 Native American language families, each different from the others. It thus appears that the first American languages diverged into the most intricately divided branch of the human language tree—within a very brief period if one accepts the Bering land bridge hypothesis.

**The Greenberg Hypothesis** Or did they? Not all linguists agree. In *Language in the Americas* (1987), Joseph Greenberg proposed that there are three families of indigenous American languages, each corresponding to a major wave of migration from Asia into the New World (Fig. 9-7). The oldest and largest and most widely distributed family is the *Amerind* superfamily, which spread from the shores of Hudson Bay to the coast of Tierra del Fuego. The next oldest, next largest, but much less widely diffused family is the *Na-Dene*, whose languages are spoken by Native Americans of northwest Canada and part of Alaska as well as by the Apache and Navajo (the outlier in the southwestern United States shown in Figure 9-7). Last to arrive in North America were speakers of the

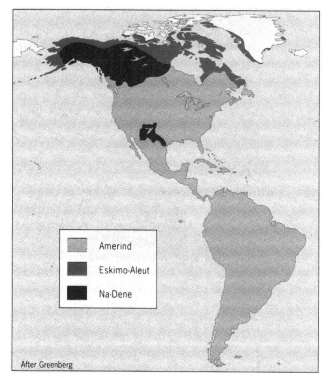

**Figure 9-7 Greenberg's Three Indigenous Language Families.** Greenberg's indigenous language families include Amerind, Eskimo-Aleut, and Na-Dene. *Source: From R. Lewin, "American Indian Language Dispute,"* Science *242, 1988, p. 1633.*

*Eskimo-Aleut* family of languages, who are still concentrated along Arctic and near-Arctic shores.

Critics of Greenberg's hypothesis contended that Greenberg did not follow proper procedures of reconstruction. Rather than studying sound shifts and other details, he compared similar-sounding words in contemporary languages. Similar work in Africa produced the map shown in Figure 8-5, which also came under heavy fire when it was first published. Today, however, that map is widely accepted.

The implications of Greenberg's hypothesis are far-reaching. If the Amerind languages are indeed members of the same family, their divergence must have occurred during a period of more than the 12,000 to 13,000 years allowed for by the dating of the first immigration. That would require a revision of the long-held view of the peopling of the Americas.

In the late 1980s and early 1990s new archeological data gave support to such a revision. A rock shelter in Pennsylvania produced artifacts dated at about 16,000 years B.P., and a site in Chile yielded material tentatively dated at 33,000 B.P. If the latter date can be confirmed, the first wave of migrants may have crossed the Pacific more than 40,000 years ago. Crucial evidence may come to light in the next several years, but at the moment the archeological evidence for very early American immigration is still tentative.

Stronger support has come from other directions. For many years Christy Turner studied dental variation among Native Americans. On the basis of dental data he concluded that the Americas were peopled in three waves of immigration that occurred over a longer period than 12,000 years. Genetic studies are also producing results consistent with the Greenberg hypothesis: the Native American speakers appear to belong to one large group whose languages have diverged over a lengthy period.

**The Continuing Controversy** A majority of linguists still doubt the three-wave hypothesis and the three-family map of American languages. They believe that the ultimate family relationships will eventually become clear from the careful reconstruction of individual languages. They also believe that drawing conclusions from the data Greenberg used is inappropriate and misleading.

Genetic research and archeological studies will ultimately resolve the issue. In the meantime we are reminded of the gaps still remaining in our knowledge—not just of the early development of humanity and its acquisition of language but even of its most recent precolonial migrations. The modern map of languages conceals a complex and fascinating past whose unraveling will help tell us not only where we were but also why we are the way we are.

# ◆ INFLUENCES ON INDIVIDUAL LANGUAGES

Each of the languages in the world's language families has its own story of origin and dispersal. We cannot hope to tell the story of even a fraction of these languages here, but we can identify some of the critical influences on the diffusion of individual tongues. First, it is clear that speakers of nonwritten languages will not retain the same language very long if they lose contact with one another. This is what led to the proliferation of languages before the advent of writing. By the same logic, the diffusion of a single tongue over a large area occurs only when people remain in contact with one another and continue to rely on a common linguistic frame of reference. Three critical components therefore have influenced the world's linguistic mosaic: writing, technology, and political organization. Writing is critical because texts are the primary means by which language can become stabilized. Technology is important because it influences both the production of written texts and the interaction of distant peoples. Political organization is key because it affects both what people have access to and which areas are in close contact with one another.

Armed with these insights, we can begin to see how the global linguistic pattern has changed. Just a few thousand years ago most habitable parts of the Earth's surface were characterized by a tremendous diversity of languages—much as one finds in interior New Guinea today. There were no literate societies and no means of bringing together peoples who were separated even by short distances. With the rise of larger-scale, more technologically sophisticated literate societies, some languages began to spread over larger areas. By two thousand years ago certain languages (notably Chinese and Latin) had successfully diffused over entire subcontinents. This was possible because these languages were associated with political systems that knit together large swaths of territory—although it should be noted that the dominant languages often coexisted with local languages that shaped the direction of regional linguistic change. Not surprisingly, then, when large-scale political systems disintegrated—as happened in the case of the Roman Empire—linguistic divergence took place.

Given the importance of writing, technology, and politics for the diffusion of languages, two developments in the late Middle Ages were of particular importance in the emergence of the modern language pattern: the invention of the printing press and the rise of nation-states. The printing press was invented in Germany in 1588, and during the next hundred years it spread to other parts of Europe and beyond. The printing press allowed for an unprecedented production of texts. Many of the early printed texts were religious, and these helped determine the standard form of various languages. The Luther Bible played this role for German, as did the King James Bible for English. The rise of nation-states was equally important, however, for these states had a strong interest in creating a more integrated state territory, and in some cases they asserted their interests in faraway places as well. Political elites thus brought peoples together and exposed them to common linguistic influences. Indeed, they played a key role in distributing printed texts. And as the leaders of countries such as England and Spain sought to expand their influence overseas, they established networks of communication and interaction that brought distant areas into closer contact than would have been conceivable just a few centuries earlier. In the process, certain languages came to be spread over vast portions of the Earth's surface.

As interesting as the historical geography of language is, the problems of language in the modern world are many and urgent. Language is a powerful component of ethnicity and lies at the heart of many current conflicts. It can be a barrier to advancement, a source of misunderstanding, and a divisive force. Governments manipulate language to bridge cultural and ethnic chasms; traders modify it to facilitate business. We consider these matters in the next chapter.

## ◆ KEY TERMS ◆

agriculture theory
Amerind
Austronesian
conquest theory
deep reconstruction
Eskimo-Aleut

Fijian
language convergence
language divergence
language replacement
Malayo-Polynesian

Na-Dene
Nostratic
Polynesian
Proto-Indo-European
sound shifts

## ◆ APPLYING GEOGRAPHIC KNOWLEDGE ◆

1. Language divergence involves the differentiation of languages over time and space. Where in North America is language divergence in progress today? What geographic factors contribute to this process here and elsewhere in the world?

2. After perhaps as long as 200,000 years of diffusion, the final phase of language dispersal (before the modern colonial period) occurred in the Americas and the Pacific. Explain how the distribution and content of indigenous languages in the Americas are analyzed to help in the reconstruction of the human settlement of this last frontier. Archeological and linguistic evidence are not always in agreement—why?

# SUPPLEMENTS

# SUPPLEMENT A. READING FOR PLEASURE

Reading for pleasure? Many ESL and developmental reading students don't think that reading can be pleasurable, or they think that reading for pleasure is a waste of time. Many reading classes, and even this book, encourage students to focus on the structures and details of academic texts—and academic material tends to be long, complex, and often boring. Let's be honest—most academic reading is anything but pleasurable! But setting aside time on a regular basis to read something fun and interesting is just as important as studying vocabulary words and learning the different ways that academic texts are structured. This supplement outlines why reading for pleasure is important and gives you ideas for adding some pleasure reading to your life—and enjoying it!

## Explanation

Reading for pleasure is a very important activity for developing your reading ability. Put most simply, you learn to read by reading! The more you read, the better you will get. The best part is, it doesn't really matter what you read as long as you read. Even reading comic books, sports magazines, or romance novels is fine, although most teachers will encourage you to read novels. So what are the advantages of reading for pleasure?

1. Pleasure reading dramatically improves overall reading comprehension. The more you read, the easier it becomes to read and understand new things you read.

2. Pleasure reading improves reading speed. One of the most difficult things about reading for ESL and other developmental readers is that reading is slow. But the more you read, the more automatic your reading process becomes, allowing you to read faster.

3. Pleasure reading builds vocabulary. When you are reading for enjoyment and focusing on a story, you actually learn new vocabulary without consciously trying.

4. Pleasure reading improves your writing. There is a clear relationship between reading and writing abilities; those who read a lot tend to be better writers.

5. Pleasure reading assists grammatical development. When you read, you learn what "sounds" right grammatically without actually studying the grammar.

6. Pleasure reading can improve your spelling.

In fact, can you guess the best way researchers have found to predict someone's reading comprehension, vocabulary level, and reading speed? You guessed it: by how much pleasure reading they do. Finding time for pleasure reading is critical if you want to quickly improve your reading abilities.

## Guidelines

To get started with pleasure reading, there are really only a few guidelines you should keep in mind.

1. Read a variety of materials on a wide range of topics (i.e., don't just read comic books).

2. You don't have to understand everything! If there is something you don't understand, skip it and keep reading.

3. Push yourself to read faster than you usually do.

4. Read in a quiet, comfortable, distraction-free area for at least fifteen minutes a day. More is better.

5. Read for pleasure. If you don't find the material interesting, put it down and start reading something else.

6. Read as much as possible.

## Activity

Pick a book or magazine that looks interesting, and then do the following.

1. Find a quiet place to read for at least fifteen minutes.

2. Read.

3. On a sheet of paper, write down how many pages you read and how long you read. Then, in a sentence or two, write down something you learned or found interesting. If it is a novel, just describe the story line. This is called a *reading log*.

4. When you finish the book, give your reading log to your teacher, or review it on your own to see what you have learned and how much you have read.

5. Try to read at least four times a week for three months, or for as long as your teacher assigns.

If you have trouble finding something interesting to read, ask your friends for suggestions. Often the things they like to read you will find interesting. You can also go to a public library and ask a librarian what books are currently popular. Usually, if you just spend time looking at books and magazines in a library, something interesting will jump out at you.

# SUPPLEMENT B. VOCABULARY DEVELOPMENT STRATEGIES: USING WORD PARTS

Good readers not only know many words, they also have a general knowledge of how words are put together. Often, when good readers come across a word they haven't seen before, they can make a good guess at its meaning because they recognize the parts that make up the word. It's worth taking the time to learn the most common word parts that occur in academic English words. When you come across a word you don't know, your knowledge of word parts may give you enough of a clue about the meaning that you can understand the word and the sentence in which it is found.

## Explanation and Examples

*Analyze the parts of the word to guess the meaning*
Chapter 1 discussed how guessing meaning from context is a useful strategy for figuring out what a word means. A second strategy is looking at the structure of the word for clues. A word can have three basic parts, and it is helpful to be able to recognize these parts in words you don't know.

1. Every word has a **base** (or stem). The base can usually stand alone as a word, like *happy*, or it can be part of a more complex word, like *happi*ness and *unhappi*ly. Many times you can figure out what a word means if you can recognize its base.

2. Many words also have a **prefix,** which is the part of a word that comes before the base. Prefixes usually add to or change the meaning of the base. For example, *happy* means "cheerful." If we add the prefix *un-*, which means "not," to create *unhappy,* the meaning changes to "not cheerful."

3. Many words may also have a **suffix,** which is the part of a word that comes after the base. Suffixes almost always change the part of speech of the base. For example, *happy* is an adjective. If we add the suffix *-ness*, the new word, *happiness,* is a noun.

You may not be able to figure out the exact meaning of a word just by looking at its parts, and many words don't have a prefix or a suffix. However, oftentimes your knowledge of word parts can help you get a general idea of what an unknown word means, especially if you combine it with what you know about the word from the context. In fact, in many cases the key clues to word meaning are found in the prefix, not the base, of a word. For example, the common science word *compound* has the base *pound,* which has many meanings, including a unit of weight or the act of hitting; but the prefix *com-* means "together" or "with," which is a better and more obvious clue to the word's meaning: something made by combining two or more parts or elements. If you know what the prefix *com-* means (together, with), you have a vital clue to the meaning of the word *compound.*

Table B.1 lists some of the most common **prefixes** in academic words, along with their most common meaning and possible alternate forms. Table B.2 lists some of the most common **suffixes** in academic words, along with their most common meanings. This table also shows the part of speech that words with this suffix usually represent.

**TABLE B.1.    Most Common Prefixes in Academic Words**

| Prefix | Common Meaning | Alternate Forms | Sample Words |
|---|---|---|---|
| be- | make | | belittle, befriend |
| com- | together, with | con-, col-, cor-, co- | combine, compete, contest, cooperate |
| de- | down, away | | detach, defrost |
| dis- | not | | dislike, disrespect |
| fore- | before, front | | forecast, forehead |
| in- | not | im-, il-, ir- | insane, impolite, illiterate, irrelevant |
| inter- | between | | interstate, intersect |
| mis- | wrong | | misspell, mistake |
| over- | above, excessive | | oversight, overload |
| out- | away from, better | | outbound, outdo |
| pre- | before | | predict, preseason |
| re- | again, back | retro- | repeat, reenact |
| sub- | under | sup-, sus- | submarine, support, sustain |
| trans- | across, beyond | | transport, transmit |
| un- | not | | unsafe, unlike |

*Source:* Data from D. Biber, S. Johansson, G. Leech, S. Conrad, and E. Finegan, *Longman Grammar of Spoken and Written English* (Essex: Longman, 1999).

**TABLE B.2.  Most Common Suffixes in Academic Words**

| Suffix | Meaning | Part of Speech | Sample Words |
|---|---|---|---|
| -(a)tion | action/instance of V-ing | Noun | realization, protection, insertion |
| -ity | state or quality of being Adj. | Noun | reliability, ability |
| -ism | Doctrine of N; movement characterized by Adj | Noun | Marxism, Buddhism capitalism, socialism |
| -ness | state or quality of being Adj. | Noun | happiness, friendliness |
| -ment | action/instance of V-ing | Noun | statement, payment, treatment |
| -ize | to make/create | Verb | specialize, modernize, stabilize |
| -en | to make/create | Verb | liven, soften, harden |
| -ate | to make/create | Verb | pollinate, differentiate |
| -(i)fy | to make/create | Verb | solidify, beautify |
| -(i)al | having nature of; related to N | Adj. | intentional, residential, medical |
| -able | able to be V-ed | Adj. | likable, teachable |
| -ent | having nature of; related to N | Adj. | different, confident |
| -ive | causing V | Adj. | restrictive, prohibitive, impressive |
| -(i)ous | having nature of; related to N | Adj. | spacious, scandalous, ridiculous |
| -ly | in this manner | Adv. | obviously, rapidly |

*Source:* Data from D. Biber, S. Johansson, G. Leech, S. Conrad, and E. Finegan, *Longman Grammar of Spoken and Written English* (Essex: Longman, 1999).

To learn these prefixes and suffixes, remember a word that contains the part. For example, to help you remember that *sub-* often means "under," remember the word *submarine,* which is something that is under water. You might find it helpful to create flash cards for these prefixes and suffixes, like the ones discussed in chapter 1.

Be careful, though, when using word parts to figure out word meaning. Because of the complexity of the English language, very often the strategy of looking at word parts *just won't work.* For example, in the word *inflammable,* one might guess from the word parts *in-* (not), *flame* (fire), and *-able* (indicates an adjective) that this word means "not able to catch fire." In fact, it has exactly the opposite meaning and is a synonym of the word *flammable!* It is always best to use word-part clues to support context clues.

## Activity

Each of the following paragraphs has one or more underlined words that you may not know. For each unknown word, use both the parts of the word and its context to figure out the meaning. Answer the following questions for each underlined word.

a. What is the base? What does the base mean?
b. Is there a prefix? If so, what is it? What does it mean?
c. Is there a suffix? If so, what is it? What part of speech does the suffix create when it ends a word? What does the suffix mean?
d. Are there context clues?
e. Can you guess what the word means?

*EXAMPLE*

Regardless of the quality of the facility, a move to a nursing home is often very stressful on the family and patient. Unfortunately, the very nature of a nursing home lends itself to experiences of <u>dislocation</u>. (Popenoe 2000, 277)

a. What is the base? <u>locate</u>

What does the base mean (if you know)? <u>find</u>

b  Is there a prefix?

If so, what is it? <u>dis-</u>

What does it mean? <u>"not" or "undo"</u>

c. Is there a suffix?

If so, what is it? <u>-ion</u>

What part of speech does it create? <u>noun</u>

What does it mean? <u>action/instance of "locating"</u>

d. Further context clues?

<u>From the context, dislocation seems to have something to do with not feeling</u>

<u>comfortable or being stressed.</u>

e. Can you guess what the word means?

<u>Dislocation is feeling like you don't belong someplace</u>

1. Similarly, to remain <u>competitive</u>, a hospital must be keenly aware of the kinds of equipment and procedures available at other [hospitals]. (Macionis 1997, 194)

a. What is the base? _____

What does the base mean? _____

b. Is there a prefix? _____

If so, what is it? _____

What does it mean? _____

c. Is there a suffix? _____

If so, what is it? _____

What part of speech does it create? _____

What does it mean? _____

d. Further context clues?

_____

_____

e. Can you guess what the word means?

_____

2. A virtual workplace . . . refers to any worksite located outside the traditional office setting where work is done. . . . Many Fortune 500 companies are <u>decentralizing</u> their operations in this way and re-creating themselves around their information networks. (Popenoe 2000, 90)

a. What is the base? _____

What does the base mean? _____

b. Is there a prefix? _____

If so, what is it? _____

What does it mean? _____

c. Is there a suffix? _____

If so, what is it? _____

What part of speech does it create? _____

What does it mean? _____

d. Further context clues?

_____

_____

e. Can you guess what the word means?

_____

3. State religion has been used to maintain social order and stratification. <u>Misfortune</u>, conquest, and slavery can be borne more easily if the oppressed believe that an afterlife holds better things. (Kottak 2000, 395)

   a. What is the base? _____

   What does the base mean? _____

   b. Is there a prefix? _____

   If so, what is it? _____

   What does it mean? _____

   c. Is there a suffix? _____

   If so, what is it? _____

   What part of speech does it create? _____

   What does it mean? _____

   d. Further context clues?

   _____

   _____

   e. Can you guess what the word means?

   _____

4. Nowhere has public <u>dissatisfaction</u> with the aims, methods, and theories of scientific forestry been greater than in the Pacific Northwest. In the last decade, the forests of this region have become the focal point of a fierce and increasingly international controversy. (Boal and Royle 1999, 50)

   a. What is the base? _____

   What does the base mean? _____

   b. Is there a prefix? _____

   If so, what is it? _____

   What does it mean? _____

   c. Is there a suffix? _____

   If so, what is it? _____

   What part of speech does it create? _____

   What does it mean? _____

   d. Further context clues?

   _____

   _____

   e. Can you guess what the word means?

   _____

5. Growth, then, may be seen as using the atoms from simple molecules to construct the complex organic molecules of an organism. Decomposition and decay may be seen as the reverse process. (Nebel and Wright 1998, 55)

   a. What is the base? _____

   What does the base mean? _____

   b. Is there a prefix? _____

   If so, what is it? _____

   What does it mean? _____

   c. Is there a suffix? _____

   If so, what is it? _____

   What part of speech does it create? _____

   What does it mean? _____

   d. Further context clues?

   _____

   _____

   e. Can you guess what the word means?

   _____

6. We have said that if we can elucidate the principles that underlie their [natural ecosystems'] sustainability, we may be able to apply those principles toward our own efforts to achieve a sustainable society. (Nebel and Wright 1998, 72)

   a. What is the base? _____

   What does the base mean? _____

   b. Is there a prefix? _____

   If so, what is it? _____

   What does it mean? _____

c. Is there a suffix? _____

If so, what is it? _____

What part of speech does it create? _____

What does it mean? _____

d. Further context clues?

_____

_____

e. Can you guess what the word means?

_____

7. For sustainability, the size of consumer populations is maintained so that overgrazing or other overuse does not occur. (Nebel and Wright 1998, 71)

a. What is the base? _____

What does the base mean? _____

b. Is there a prefix? _____

If so, what is it? _____

What does it mean? _____

c. Is there a suffix? _____

If so, what is it? _____

What part of speech does it create? _____

What does it mean? _____

d. Further context clues?

_____

_____

e. Can you guess what the word means?

_____

# SUPPLEMENT C. ADDITIONAL VOCABULARY IDENTIFICATION PRACTICE

Chapter 1 and supplement A offer strategies for using the context of the sentence and the meaning of prefixes and suffixes to figure out the meaning of words you may not know. Chapter 2 outlines strategies for recognizing technical terms and their definitions. Supplement C provides more practice with all of these strategies.

**Practice**

Each of the following paragraphs has one or two underlined words that you may not know. For each underlined word, use parts of the word and its context in the sentence to figure out the meaning. Explain how you guessed this meaning.

1. Certain human <u>collectivities</u> are not groups in the sociological sense because they have no social structure at all. An example is people who merely share a particular social <u>trait</u>: liberals or conservatives, females or males, high school or college graduates. (Popenoe 2000, 84)

   a. <u>collectivities</u>:

      Guessed meaning: _____

      Clues to meaning: _____

   b. <u>trait</u>

      Guessed meaning: _____

      Clues to meaning: _____

2. As we noted earlier, our available resources always fall short of our output desires. The central problem here again is <u>scarcity</u>, a situation where our desires for goods and services exceed our capacity to produce them. (Schiller 2002, 4)

Guessed meaning: _____

Clues to meaning: _____

3. If you had no concern for future jobs or income, there would be little point in doing homework now. You might as well party all day if you're that present-oriented. On the other hand, if you value future jobs and income, it makes sense to <u>allocate</u> some present time to studying. Then you'll have more human capital (knowledge and skills) later to pursue job opportunities. (Schiller 2002, 11)

Guessed meaning: _____

Clues to meaning: _____

4. Varen <u>differentiated</u> two approaches to geography. One he called "special geography." . . . Varen defined a second approach to geography that he called "general geography." (Bergman 1995, 3)

Guessed meaning: _____

Clues to meaning: _____

## More Practice: Technical Terms

In the following sentences and short paragraphs, circle the technical terms or concepts that are defined and then underline the definition. Describe the textual clues that identify the technical terms and definitions.

1. Another familiar social grouping is the ethnic group. An *ethnic group* consists of people who share a common social and cultural background and feeling of identity with each other. (Popenoe 2000, 85)

2. This chapter introduces the world's **population geography,** that is, the distribution of humankind across the Earth. (Bergman 1995, 122)

3. It is often thought that a place's population density reflects the productivity of the local environment. Some scholars differentiate **arithmetic density**—the number of people per unit of area—from **physiological density**—the density of population per unit of arable land. (Bergman 1995, 123)

4. Some writers argue that variations in the physical environment explain even the variations among human cultures. Theories that emphasize the role of the environment in human life are called environmentalist theories. (Bergman 1995, 46)

# SUPPLEMENT D. ADDITIONAL LIST OF COMMON ACADEMIC VOCABULARY

Table 1.1 lists 300 of the most common academic words. Table D.1 provides an additional 270 common academic words that students need to know and know how to use, along with their related forms. These two groups of words make up 10 percent of the words used in academic textbooks.

**TABLE D.1. 270 Additional Common Academic Words** (Adapted from Coxhead 2000)

The different forms of these words should be learned as well. For example, when learning *adapt,* you should also learn *adapts, adapting,* and *adaptable.*

| | | | |
|---|---|---|---|
| **A** | appreciate | channel | confirm |
| abandon | arbitrary | chart | conform |
| abstract | assemble | chemical | contemporary |
| accommodate | assign | cite | contradict |
| accompany | assure | clarify | contrary |
| accumulate | attach | classic | controversy |
| accurate | attain | coherent | converse |
| acknowledge | author | coincide | convert |
| adapt | automate | collapse | convince |
| adjacent | | colleague | cooperate |
| adult | **B** | commence | couple |
| advocate | behalf | commodity | crucial |
| aggregate | bias | compatible | currency |
| aid | bond | compile | |
| albeit | brief | complement | **D** |
| allocate | bulk | comprehensive | decade |
| ambiguous | | comprise | definite |
| analogy | **C** | conceive | denote |
| anticipate | capable | concurrent | deny |
| append | cease | confine | depress |

148

**TABLE D.1—*Continued***

| | | | |
|---|---|---|---|
| detect | grade | mediate | **R** |
| deviate | guarantee | medium | radical |
| device | guideline | migrate | random |
| devote | | military | rational |
| differentiate | **H** | minimal | recover |
| diminish | hierarchy | minimize | refine |
| discriminate | highlight | minimum | reinforce |
| displace | | ministry | relax |
| display | **I** | mode | release |
| dispose | identical | motive | reluctance |
| distort | ideology | mutual | restore |
| diverse | ignorance | | restrain |
| domain | implicit | **N** | reveal |
| drama | incentive | neutral | reverse |
| duration | incidence | nevertheless | revise |
| dynamic | incline | nonetheless | revolution |
| | incorporate | norm | rigid |
| **E** | index | notwithstanding | route |
| edit | induce | nuclear | |
| eliminate | inevitable | | **S** |
| empirical | infer | **O** | scenario |
| encounter | infrastructure | odd | schedule |
| enhance | inherent | offset | scope |
| enormous | inhibit | ongoing | simulate |
| equip | initiate | overlap | so-called |
| erode | innovate | overseas | sole |
| estate | input | | somewhat |
| ethic | insert | **P** | sphere |
| eventual | insight | panel | straightforward |
| exceed | inspect | paradigm | submit |
| exhibit | instruct | paragraph | subordinate |
| expert | integral | passive | subsidy |
| explicit | integrity | persist | successor |
| exploit | intelligence | phenomenon | supplement |
| extract | intense | plus | survive |
| | intermediate | portion | suspend |
| **F** | interval | pose | |
| federal | intervene | practitioner | **T** |
| fee | intrinsic | precede | tape |
| file | invoke | predominant | team |
| finite | isolate | preliminary | temporary |
| flexible | | presume | tense |
| fluctuate | **L** | priority | terminate |
| format | lecture | prohibit | theme |
| forthcoming | levy | prospect | thereby |
| found | likewise | protocol | thesis |
| foundation | | publication | topic |
| furthermore | **M** | | trace |
| | manipulate | **Q** | transform |
| **G** | manual | qualitative | transmit |
| gender | mature | quote | transport |
| globe | media | | trigger |

*(continued)*

**TABLE D.1—*Continued***

| U | unique | violate | W |
|---|---|---|---|
| ultimate | utilize | virtual | whereby |
| undergo | | visible | widespread |
| underlie | V | vision | |
| uniform | vehicle | visual | |
| unify | via | voluntary | |

*Source:* Adapted from A. Coxhead, "A New Academic Word List," *TESOL Quarterly* 34, no. 2 (2000): 213–38.

Once you've learned the words given in chapter 1, make flash cards and begin reviewing the words in table D.1 using the technique outlined in chapter 1.

1. Make flash cards for 25 of the words that you already know and feel comfortable using, and then review them.

2. For each of the words you wrote in step 1 above, on a separate sheet of paper first write the definition; then write an original sentence using the word so that it clearly shows that you understand what the word means and how to use it. Underline the word in the sentence. If you know more than one meaning for the word, give an example for both meanings. See if you can do this without looking at your flash card.

### EXAMPLE

A. *occupy* (verb): to be, live, or work in a place.

That company is very large. Its offices <u>occupy</u> three city blocks.

B. *cóntrast* (noun): a comparison between two things that shows a difference.

Although they are brothers, most people think they are from different families. The <u>contrast</u> in how they look, talk, and dress is amazing.

*contrást* (verb): to differ; to analyze the differences

The speaker was very interesting. She was <u>contrasting</u> life in the United States with life in Peru.

3. Each week, make a new set of flash cards for another twenty-five words from the list in table D.1 until you have made a flash card for all of the words listed. Add these new cards to your flash card pile and review them all regularly, at least once a day if possible. Your goal is to be able to "automatically" recognize the words and how they are used without having to stop and think about them.

4. For each new set of twenty-five words for which you create flash cards, repeat step 2 above once you feel you have learned the word. Repeat weekly until you feel comfortable with using them.

5. As you read and come across other new words you (or your teacher) think you should learn, make flash cards for them, too, and add them to your review pile.

6. After a couple of weeks, put aside the cards for words that you feel you know well and focus on the ones that you still need to learn. At a later date, review these cards again to see if you still remember them. If you don't, put them back in your active review pile.

# SUPPLEMENT E. ADDITIONAL MAIN IDEAS AND ORGANIZATIONAL STRUCTURE PRACTICE

The following paragraphs have been taken from typical introductory-level textbooks in a variety of fields. Each has a main idea, as discussed in chapter 5, and each uses one or more of the organizational structures described in chapters 6, 7, and 8. For each of the following, (1) determine the main idea of the passage, (2) determine which organizational structure or structures are used to develop the ideas, (3) note any words that signal the structure, and (4) draw a diagram or make an outline that shows the relationship of the ideas in the paragraphs.

## EXAMPLE

Amitai Etzioni (1975) has identified three types of formal organizations, distinguished by why people participate—utilitarian organizations, normative organizations, and coercive organizations. . . .

Just about everyone who works for income is a member of a *utilitarian organization,* which provides material rewards for its members. Large business enterprises, for example, generate profits for their owners and income in the form of salaries and wages for their employees. . . .

People join *normative organizations* not for income but to pursue goals they consider morally worthwhile. . . . These include community service groups, political parties, religious organizations, and numerous other confederations concerned with specific social issues. . . .

In Etzioni's typology, *coercive organizations* are distinguished by involuntary membership. That is, people are forced to join the organization as a form of punishment (prisons) or treatment (psychiatric hospitals). (Macionis 1997, 185)

a. *Main idea:* Three types of formal organizations, distinguished by why people participate.

b. These paragraphs use primarily classification structure (three types) but also have an implied compare-contrast organization (distinguished by).

c. Word cues: "types," "distinguished by"

d. Types of formal organizations and why people participate

   1. Utilitarian (provides material rewards)
      (contrasted with)

   2. Normative (address moral or social issues)
      (contrasted with)

   3. Coercive (forced group membership)

1. Regular seasonal changes in climate, which influence the seasonal availability of resources, have significant effects on subsistence strategies [or food-getting strategies]. Subsistence strategies also develop in response to unpredictable, short-term changes in the environment (drought, floods, or diseases that affect animals) that recur over the long run.

   The most important effect on subsistence strategies, however, is long-run environmental uncertainty. For example, most societies adapt their food habits and preferences to a wide variety of resources, rather than limiting themselves to only one or two. (Nanda and Warms 1998, 108)

2. When a sample of water is completely evaporated, the crystals of any solid substance that was dissolved in the water are left behind. These crystals may be of three types. (1) The crystals may be a pure solid. No water remains in these crystals. (2) The crystals may contain water mechanically enclosed within the crystal. The amount of water thus enclosed can vary. (3) The crystals may be made up of the solid substance combined chemically with water in a definite ratio. The third type is called a **hydrate.** (Dorin, Demmin, and Gabel 1992, 287)

3. Most important for our discussion, however, is the fact that every stage of the energy conversion process—from discovery, to extraction, processing, and utilization—has an impact on the physical landscape. In the coalfields of the world, from the U.S. Appalachian Mountains to western Siberia, mining results in a loss of vegetation and topsoil, erosion, and water pollution, acid and toxic drainage. It also contributes to cancer and lung disease in coal miners. . . . The burning of coal is associated with relatively high emissions of environmentally harmful gases such as carbon dioxide and sulfur dioxide. (Knox and Marston 1998, 172)

4. The Earth contains six major environmental zones, each of which has a particular climate, soil composition, and plant and animal life. Approximately one-quarter of the Earth's surface is covered by **grasslands,** sometimes called steppes, prairies, or savannas. These areas, which can support hunters and gatherers and also populations dependent on herding animals, are inhabited by 10% of the world's population. With complex machine technologies, these areas can be enormously productive for agriculture.

   **Deserts** or dry regions make up 18% of the Earth's land but contain only 6% of its population. Not all deserts conform to the popular image of sand dunes and the complete absence of water. Many deserts are covered with brush, and in some areas, oases, or fertile concentrations of soil, support small agricultural settlements. Desert plant and animal life can sometimes support hunters and gatherers. With extensive irrigation, some deserts can even support intensive agriculture and dense populations.

The Arctic and subarctic zones cover 16% of the Earth, but as we would expect, they support only a tiny fraction of the Earth's population—less than half of 1%—who mainly live by hunting, herding, and trapping.

Approximately three-quarters of the world's population lives in the . . . remaining major environmental zones. The **tropical forest** zone, with abundant rainfall and luxuriant vegetation, takes up 10% of the Earth's land mass but supports 28% of its population. The typical pattern of subsistence in these areas is extensive cultivation (sometimes called horticulture). Today, the most populous environmental zone is the **temperate forest,** which supports almost half the world's population.

Mountains, which vary in climate and other characteristics according to their elevation, occupy 12% of the Earth's land surface and are inhabited by 7% of its population, engaged primarily in pastoralism and extensive cultivation. (Nanda and Warms 1998, 107–8)

5. The formative period in the area around Teotihuacán (1000–300 B.C.) was characterized initially by small, scattered farming villages on the hilly slopes just south of the Teotihuacán Valley [Mexico]. There were probably a few hundred people in each hamlet, and each of these scattered groups was probably politically autonomous. After about 500 B.C., there seems to have been a population shift to settlements on the valley floor, probably in association with the use of irrigation. Between about 300 and 200 B.C. small "elite" centers emerged in the valley; each had an earthen or stone raised platform. Residences or small temples of poles and thatch originally stood on these platforms. That some individuals, particularly those in the elite centers, were buried in special tombs supplied with ornaments, headdresses, carved bowls, and a good deal of food indicates some social inequality. The various elite centers may indicate the presence of chiefdoms. (Ember and Ember 2000, 134)

6. In 264 B.C., Rome and Carthage went to war for control of Sicily and the western Mediteranean. Thus began the first of three periods of struggle known as the Punic (**PYOO**-nik) Wars. *Punic* comes from the Latin word for Phonecia.

Let us compare the two cities and their capacity for making war. With a population of 250,000, Carthage was about three times the size of Rome. Carthage had a huge navy of 500 ships. Overseas trade had made Carthage an immensely wealthy city. Each year, it collected the equivalent of almost 1 million pounds of gold in tariffs and tribute. With this great wealth, Carthage employed the people of neighboring Numidia as **mercenaries,** soldiers who fight in any country's army for pay.

Rome's resources in ships and wealth seemed meager by comparison. In fact, at the beginning of the First Punic War, Rome had no navy whatsoever. Rome's power had always rested entirely on its armies. However, this great disadvantage was offset by three advantages. First, Rome could draw on a reserve of more than 500,000 troops made available through its conquests in Italy. Second, Rome's citizen troops were generally more loyal and reliable than the mercenaries employed by Carthage. Third, warfare was a Roman specialty. Over the centuries, Romans had directed much of their energy toward winning wars. All of Carthage's energies, on the other hand, had been aimed at winning wealth through trade. (Krieger, Neill, and Reynolds 1997, 137–8)

7. In the middle 1200's, a fierce group of horsemen from central Asia slashed their way into Russia. These nomads were the Mongols. . . . In 1240, they completely destroyed Kiev. Its churches were burned, its rich treasures were plundered, and even its tombs were broken open and the bones scattered. By 1241, the Mongols ruled all of Russia. From that time on, Russian history followed a new course. (Krieger, Neill, and Reynolds 1997, 265)

8. [The following excerpt is from an electrical engineering course. Even if you don't understand it completely, you should be able to pick out the main idea and determine the organizational pattern used.] A systematic method of converting whole numbers from decimal to binary is the *repeated division-by-2* process. For example, to convert the decimal number 12 to binary, begin by dividing 12 by 2. Then divide each resulting quotient by 2 until there is a 0 whole-number quotient. The **remainders** generated by each division form the binary number. (Floyd 2000, 46)

9. When you perform a Yahoo! search, Yahoo! will actually perform three searches. It first searches its own directory of category names. Then it searches its own directory of websites listed in Yahoo! Finally, it searches webpages indexed by an outside search engine, Inktomi. The results it returns to you are divided into three lists. (Branscomb 2001, 75–76)

10. We can describe who's who in the business community, then, in two very different ways. In terms of numbers, the single proprietorship is the most common type of business firm in America. Proprietorships are particularly dominant in agriculture (the family farm), retail trade (the corner grocery store), and services (your dentist). In terms of size, however, the corporation is the dominant force in the U.S. economy . . . The four largest nonfinancial corporations in the country (GE, Ford, Exxon, Wal-Mart) alone have more assets than *all* the 15 million proprietorships doing business in the United States. (Schiller 2002, 43)

11. There is a clear connection between sweets and ***dental caries*** (tooth decay). People who eat much sugar are likely to have a higher incidence of tooth decay than people who eat less sugar. However, sugar is not the only culprit. Starches can promote tooth decay, too.

Bacteria that live in the mouth feed on the carbohydrates in food particles. The bacteria form a sticky substance called *plaque* that clings to teeth. As the bacteria grow, they produce acid that eats away the protective tooth enamel, forming pits in the teeth. In time, these pits can deepen into cavities.

The risk of dental caries depends on two main factors: the type of food and when you eat it. Sticky, carbohydrate foods, like raisins, cookies, crackers, and caramels, tend to cling to teeth. They are more harmful than foods that are quickly swallowed and removed from contact with the teeth. Likewise, sugars and starches eaten between meals tend to be more harmful to tooth enamel than carbohydrates consumed at meals. This is because particles from between-meal snacks tend to remain in the mouth for longer periods. Carbohydrates eaten during meals are removed from the mouth by beverages and other foods eaten with them. (West 2000, 85)

12. About 1 million years ago, huge glaciers covered the northern regions of the Americas, and many areas that are now under water were then dry land. One of these areas was a narrow land bridge that joined Siberia, the easternmost part of Asia, with Alaska, the westernmost part of the Americas.

   It was this land bridge that the ancestors of the American Indians used, about 20,000 to 30,000 years ago, to cross from Asia to the Americas. They came in small bands, a few at a time, over the next several thousand years. . . .

   About 10,000 years later, Earth's climate turned warmer and drier. Slowly water from melting glaciers raised the level of the oceans and the land bridge joining Asia and the Americas disappeared, covered by a body of water. . . . With the bridge gone, Asian migrations to the Americas ended.

   The descendants of the original migrants spread over wide areas, moving from North America into Central America and, by 11,000 B.C., from there to the southern tip of South America . . . In time there were thousands of separate tribes, each speaking a different language and following its own way of life.

   About 5000 B.C. there was a new development, one that changed the ways American Indians lived. Food gatherers in the region north of Central America known as Mexico began growing **maize** (mayz), or corn. . . . They learned how to plant and cultivate a number of other crops as well—beans, squash, pumpkins, cotton, and sweet potatoes. With a better food supply, the Indians could settle down in villages and develop arts and crafts. (Farah and Karls 1990, 196–7)

13. The flood of the Tigris and the Euphrates, unlike that of the Nile, cannot be predicted. It may come anytime between the beginning of April and the early part of June. Not only is the exact time of year unpredictable, but the extent of the flood cannot be estimated. Not surprisingly, the people of the valley viewed nature and the gods as angry and unreasonable. Their world differed greatly from that of the Egyptians, who generally saw only goodness in nature. (Mazour and Peoples 1990, 28)

14. The rest of the people of France—approximately 97 percent—belonged to the Third Estate. This estate was itself subdivided into three goups.

   At the top stood the **bourgeoisie** (boorzh • wah • ZEE)—the city-dwelling middle class—made up of merchants, manufacturers, and professional people such as doctors and lawyers. Many of them possessed wealth and education. Below the bourgeoisie came the laborers and artisans of the cities. The peasants ranked at the bottom of the Third Estate and often lived miserable lives, mired in inescapable poverty. (Mazour and Peoples 1990, 425)

# REFERENCES

Akmajian, A., R. Demers, A. Farmer, and R. Harnish. 1995. *Linguistics: An Introduction to Language and Communication.* 4th ed. Cambridge: MIT Press.

Bergman, E. F. 1995. *Human Geography: Cultures, Connections, and Landscapes.* Englewood Cliffs, NJ: Prentice-Hall.

Biber, D., S. Johansson, G. Leech, S. Conrad, and E. Finegan. 1999. *Longman Grammar of Spoken and Written English.* Essex: Longman.

Boal, F. W., and S. Royle, eds. 1999. *North America: A Geographical Mosaic.* New York: Oxford University Press.

Branscomb, H. E. 2001. *Casting Your Net: A Student's Guide to Research on the Internet.* 2d ed. Boston: Allyn and Bacon.

Celce-Murcia, M., and D. Larsen-Freeman. 1983. *The Grammar Book: An ESL/EFL Teacher's Course.* Rowley, Mass.: Newbury House Publishers.

Coxhead, A. "A New Academic Word List." 2000. *TESOL Quarterly* 34, no. 2: 213–38.

de Blij, H. J., and A. B. Murphy. 1999. *Human Geography: Culture, Society, and Space.* 6th ed. New York: John Wiley and Sons.

Dorin, H., P. E. Demmin, and D. L. Gabel. 1992. *Chemistry: The Study of Matter.* 4th ed. Needham, Mass.: Prentice-Hall.

Ember, C. R., and M. Ember. 2000. *Anthropology: A Brief Introduction.* 4th ed. Upper Saddle River, N.J.: Prentice-Hall.

Farah, M., and A. B. Karls. 1990. *The Human Experience: A World History.* Columbus, Ohio: Merrill Publishing.

Floyd, T. L. 2000. *Digital Fundamentals.* 7th ed. Upper Saddle River, N.J.: Prentice-Hall.

Freund, J. E. 2001. *Modern Elementary Statistics.* 10th ed. Upper Saddle River, N.J.: Prentice-Hall.

Glover, J. A., and R. H. Bruning. 1987. *Educational Psychology: Principles and Applications.* 2d ed. Boston: Little, Brown.

Hiebert, P. G. 1983. *Cultural Anthropology.* Grand Rapids: Baker Book House.

Howell, D. C. 1987. *Statistical Methods for Psychology.* 2d ed. Boston: Duxbury Press.

Jordan-Bychkov, T. G., and M. Domosh. 1999. *The Human Mosaic.* 8th ed. New York: Addison Wesley Longman.

Knox, P. L., and S. A. Marston. 1998. *Places and Regions in Global Context: Human Geography.* Upper Saddle River, NJ: Prentice-Hall.

Kottack, C. P. 2000. *Anthropology: The Exploration of Human Diversity.* 8th ed. Boston: McGraw-Hill.

Krieger, L. S., K. Neill, and E. Reynolds. 1997. *World History: Perspectives on the Past.* 5th ed. Lexington: D.C. Heath.

Macionis, J. J. 1997. *Sociology.* 6th ed. Upper Saddle River, N.J.: Prentice-Hall.

Mazour, A. G., and J. M. Peoples. 1990. *World History: People and Nations.* Orlando: Harcourt Brace Jovanovich.

Medin, D. L., and B. H. Ross. 1992. *Cognitive Psychology.* Fort Worth: Harcourt Brace Jovanovich College Publishers.

Miller, K. R., and J. Levine. 1998a. *Biology: The Living Science—Animals.* Upper Saddle River, N.J.: Prentice-Hall.

Miller, K. R., and J. Levine. 1998b. *Biology: The Living Science—The Human Body.* Upper Saddle River, NJ: Prentice-Hall.

Nanda, S., and R. L. Warms. 1998. *Cultural Anthropology.* 6th ed. Belmont, Calif.: Wadsworth.

Nation, I. S. P. 1990. *Teaching and Learning Vocabulary.* New York: Newbury House.

Nebel, B. J., and R. T. Wright. 1998. *Environmental Science.* 6th ed. Upper Saddle River, N.J.: Prentice-Hall.

O'Grady, W., M. Dobrovolsky, and M. Aronoff. 1997. *Contemporary Linguistics.* 3d ed. New York: St. Martin's Press.

Popenoe, D. 2000. *Sociology.* Upper Saddle River, N.J.: Prentice-Hall.

Pressley, M., and P. Afflerbach. 1995. *Verbal Protocols of Reading: The Nature of Constructively Responsive Reading.* Hillsdale, N.J.: Lawrence Erlbaum Associates.

Rings, S. R., and J. F. Kremer. 2000. *Introductory Psychology: Psychology as a Social Science.* Indianapolis: Department of Psychology, Indiana University–Purdue University Indianapolis.

Saffell, D. C. 1996. *Civics: Responsibilities and Citizenship.* New York: Glencoe/McGraw-Hill.

Sanders, M. 1997. *Communication Technology: Today and Tomorrow.* 2d ed. New York: Glencoe McGraw-Hill.

Schaefer, R. T. 2000. *Sociology: A Brief Introduction.* 3d ed. Boston: McGraw-Hill Higher Education.

Schaefer, R. T., and R. P. Lamm. 1995. *Sociology.* 5th ed. New York: McGraw-Hill.

Schiller, B. R. 2002. *Essentials of Economics.* 4th ed. Boston: McGraw-Hill Irwin.

Thill, J. V., and C. L. Bovée. 1993. *Excellence in Business Communication.* 2d ed. New York: McGraw-Hill.

Thomas, E., et al. 1998. "Ground Zero." *Newsweek,* 25 May.

West, D. F. 2000. *Nutrition and Fitness: Lifestyle Choices for Wellness.* Tinley Park, Ill.: Gooheart-Wilcox.

# ANSWER KEY

**Chapter 1**  Activity

1–4: Answers will vary. Sample response for 1 is given below.

A. <u>relocation</u> is a noun, <u>relocating</u> is a verb (gerund); B. An employee is relocating from one town to another; C. <u>relocating</u> is an action and involves someone coming from "out of town"; D. relocating is when someone <u>moves</u> from one location to another location; E. "move" and "moving" can be substituted and make sense: ". . . coordinate the person's <u>move</u>," ". . . procedures for <u>moving</u> employees."

**Dictionary definition:** to relocate means to move to a new place.

Putting It into Practice

Part 1. Answers will vary. Nontechnical words that many students may not know might include *fundamental, reveal, enable, innumerable, composed, analogous, constituent, diminish, various, essential, distinction,* and *implies.*

Part 2. Answers will vary depending on the text used. Nontechnical words that many students may not know from the first page of the chapter in appendix 2 include *patchwork, divergence, centuries, derivative, retrace, elusive, relevance, respectively, feasible, yielded, resemblance,* and *predictable.*

**Chapter 2**  Activity

1. secondary group. Clues: the term is in bold; the linking verb *is* is used; the definition is given in italics.
2. dendrites. Clues: the term is in bold; an appositive occurs immediately after the term, separated by a hyphen.
3. cultural relativism. Clue: the term is followed by an appositive (which is not marked by *which, that,* or a dash).
4. a. semi-structured interviews. Clue: the term is followed by a restatement, "that is"; b. structured interviews. Clue: the term is followed by an appositive ("ones in which . . .").
5. hydrologists. Clue: the term is followed by a clarifying term in parentheses "(water experts)".
6. a. infiltration. Clues: the term is in bold and is an appositive renaming the previous clause, "soak into the ground." b. runoff. Clues: the term is in bold and is an appositive renaming the previous clause, "run off the surface." c. watershed. Clues: the term is in bold; it is connected to its definition by the defining verb "is referred to."
7. productivity. Clues: the term is in bold and is an appositive following a hyphen.
8. socially prescribed role. Clues: the term is followed by a dash and the restatement "that is."

9. desertification. Clues: the term is in bold and is followed by the defining verb "to refer to."
10. human capital. Clue: the term is defined by the following parenthetical phrase: (knowledge and skills).

### Putting It into Practice

Part 1. Answers will vary. Possible answers might include the following.

1. Parentheses: (Carbohydrates) (sugars and starches), and fats can be oxidized easily by the body to provide energy. (p. 63) Clue: the terms in parentheses immediately follow the technical term.
2. Bold or italics: (Kinetic energy) is *energy in action or motion* (p. 56). Clues: the term is bold, is followed by the linking verb "is", and the definition is in italics.
3. Defining verbs: (Inorganic), then, refers to molecules or compounds with neither carbon-carbon nor carbon-hydrogen bonds (p. 55). Clues: the term is in bold and is followed by the defining verb "refers to."
4. Appositive: One of the most common units is the (calorie), which is defined as the *amount of heat required to raise the temperature of 1 gram (1 milliliter) of water 1 degree Celsius* (p. 59). Clues: the term is in bold, it is followed by the appositive "which is. . .", and the definition is in italics.
5. Restatement: In nature, (anaerobic), or *oxygen-free*, environments commonly exist in the sediment at the bottom of marshes or swamps . . . (p. 66). Clues: the term is in bold and the definition is preceded by the word "or," is separated by commas, and is in italics.
6. Delayed definition: In a grazing situation it is readily apparent that if the animals eat the grass faster than the grass can regrow, sooner or later the grass will be destroyed and all the animals will starve. This situation is known as (overgrazing) (p. 71). Clues: the term is in bold and follows the defining verb "is known as."

## Chapter 3    Activity

1. "Nowhere is this . . ." "This" refers to religion's influence on "the way people perceive their physical environment."
2. "Such temporary disruptions . . ." This restates the idea of awakening during the night and being uncertain where you are.
3. "These, in turn, enable . . ." The ideas being referred back to are the clothes and houses humans use to create artificial environments.
4. "This example demonstrates . . ." The idea being referred back to is comparison of where German-speaking people and Italians tend to live in the Alps.
5. ". . . these fundamental differences in the farming practices . . ." The idea being referred back to is the differences in reliance on inanimate power and agricultural machines between Amish and non-Amish farmers.
6. "This instrument . . ." The idea being referred back to is a digital multimeter.

### Putting It into Practice

Part 1. Answers will vary. Possible answers might include the following.
1. "Our look at this basic level will reveal underlying principles that enable . . ." (p. 51). "This basic level" refers back to the idea in the previous sentence, "the fundamental level of chemicals and energy."
2. "Only 92 different kinds of atoms occur in nature, and these are known as . . ." (p. 52). "These" refers back to the "92 different kinds of atoms" that occur in nature.
3. "This constancy of atoms is regarded as a fundamental natural law . . ." (p. 52). "This constancy of atoms" refers back to the ideas in the previous two sentences that atoms do not change, nor are new ones created and destroyed in chemical reactions.

## Chapter 4    Activity

Part 1
1. a    3. b
2. a    4. a

Part 2

2. **and:** Indicates <u>additional</u> information identifying which organizations are the ones in which sexual harassment usually occurs.

3. **— . . . —:** Provides <u>clarification</u> of which type of women are commonly victims of sexual harassment.

4. **While:** Shows <u>contrast</u> between the idea that there is widespread sexual harassment and the idea that it is not typically reported.

5. **nevertheless:** Supporting "while" above, also shows <u>contrast</u> between the idea that there is widespread sexual harassment and the idea that it is not typically reported.

6. **For example:** Indicates that an <u>example</u> is being given of sexual harassment not being reported.

7. **After:** Emphasis on <u>when</u> (in a sequence of time—at the end of nine years) Broderick won her court case.

8. **Still:** Indicates a <u>contrast</u> emphasizing that although Broderick won her case, it was a very difficult legal battle.

9. **Even if:** shows <u>condition;</u> in this case emphasizing how difficult the legal process is.

10. **or:** Shows <u>alternatives</u> (contrast) indicating that neither the courts or other bureaucracies quickly deal with sexual harassment complaints.

11. **";":** By using the semicolon, the writer indicates that the following sentence will provide <u>clarification</u> of the previous sentence, showing how "huge" the caseload is with specific numbers.

12. **and also:** Indicates <u>additional</u> information is being given about how huge the caseload is.

13. **Yet:** Shows <u>contrast</u> indicating that the funding is not adequate to deal with the huge caseload.

14. **however:** Emphasizes the <u>contrast</u>, that lack of money is not the only problem.

## Putting It into Practice

Part 1. Answers will vary. Possible answers might include the following.

1. <u>Also,</u> understanding at this level will provide a background for understanding . . . (p. 51). "Also" indicates that an <u>additional</u> reason is being given for looking at how ecosystems work at the fundamental level of chemicals and energy.

2. All chemical reactions, <u>whether</u> they occur in a test tube, in the environment, <u>or</u> inside living things. . . . (p. 52). "Whether . . . or" indicates a list of options, or <u>conditions,</u> that lead to a similar result.

3. A carbon atom, <u>for instance,</u> will always remain a carbon atom (p. 52). "For instance" indicates that an <u>example</u> is being given of how atoms do not change when different materials are being put together or taken apart.

4. <u>Thus,</u> air is a source of carbon, oxygen, and nitrogen for all organisms (p. 52). "Thus" indicates a <u>result or effect</u>—because carbon, oxygen, and nitrogen are found in air, the air is an important source of these gases for organisms.

**Chapter 5**

## Activity 1

1. a. S,    b. M,    c. S,    d. T
2. a. S,    b. T,    c. M,    d. S
3. a. T,    b. S,    c. M,    d. S

## Activity 2

1. Topic: How the human nervous system works. Main idea: "The human nervous system is similar to a complex telephone network in a large city."

2. Topic: The development of health psychology and behavioral medicine. Main idea: "Health psychology and behavioral medicine have experienced tremendous growth since their beginnings in the early 1970s."

3. Topic: The development of human communities and civilizations. Main idea: The domestication of animals and development of new weapons "undoubtedly helped human communities and civilizations to develop."

4. Topic: Disadvantages of two-party systems. Main idea: "Two-party systems are not without disadvantages."

5. Topic: Role of instincts in animal survival. Main idea: "In lower animals, where instincts rather than culture guide social life, the young can function independently at a very early age."

## Putting It into Practice

### Part 1a

1. First sentence: "chemical reactions also involve the absorption or release of energy."
2. Second sentence: "a more technical definition of matter . . ."
3. Last clause of third sentence: "it is practical to consider them as the basic units of matter."
4. Implied: what is energy [See also last sentence: "energy is the ability to move matter."]
5. First sentence: "Energy is commonly divided into two major categories: *kinetic* and *potential*."
6. First sentence: "Energy may be changed from one form to another in innumerable ways."
7. Implied: How we measure energy
8. First sentence: "We define energy as the ability to move matter."

### Part 1b

1. The laws of thermodynamics
2. The main idea is implied. It is that there are two laws of thermodynamics that govern energy conversion and movement.
3. The first paragraph describes the first law. The second paragraph describes the second law. The third through fifth paragraphs further explain the second law.

## Chapter 6     Activity

1. Main idea: Different ways that ethnic groups relate to each other.
   Organizational markers: "One," "is another," "more typical," "four identifiable patterns," (1)–(4).
   Outline

   Different ways ethnic groups relate to each other
     Extreme behaviors
       a. genocide
       b. expulsion
     Typical relations
       c. amalgmation
       d. assimilation
       e. segregation
       f. pluralism

2. Main idea: Ways of describing population movement.
   Organizational markers: "One way," "The second way."
   Outline

   Ways of describing population movement
     a. mobility
     b. migration
       1. emigration
       2. immigration

3. Main idea: Reasons why we like certain foods and dislike others.
   Organizational markers: "one factor," "too."
   Outline

   Reasons why we like certain foods and dislike others
     a. emotions
     b. genes
     c. experiences

4. Main idea: The last three geological eras.
   Organizational markers: "the oldest," "the middle era," ". . . ; and . . ."
   Outline

   The last three geological eras
      a. Paleozoic
      b. Mesozoic
      c. Cenozoic

**Chapter 7**   Activity

Part 1
1. Words that indicate comparison/contrast: no specific words used; contrast is implied. Push factors are being contrasted with pull factors based on the reasons why migration occurs and the origin of those reasons.
2. Words that indicate comparison/contrast: "more than," "can be much, much larger," "are far more powerful than." Also verb tense (past tense/present tense). Early computers are being contrasted with modern computers based on what they can/cannot do.
3. Words that indicate comparison/contrast: "better," "new methods," "But other far more important changes," "however." The New Stone Age is being contrasted with the Old and Middle Stone Age based on how people made tools and how they lived.
4. Words that indicate comparison/contrast: "Different," "however," "Similar contrasts," "easier," "than it was," "Some," "Others," "Still others," "Finally, a few." Territorial characteristics are contrasted with other territorial characteristics based on the opportunities and challenges they present.

Part 2
1. The "old" nuclear club is being contrasted with the "new" nuclear club based on the stability that these two arrangements offered.
2. Warranted claim is being contrasted with unwarranted claim based on how they are supported by fact (truth).

**Chapter 8**   Activity

1. Organizational pattern: cause-effect (enumeration)
   Main idea: The effect that stress has on health
   Diagram

   Stress   →   Physical illness
                    —heart disease
                    —hardening of arteries
                    —diabetes
   (Cause)        (Effect)

2. Organizational pattern: cause-effect (enumeration and contrast)
   Main idea: The reasons why birds can fly
   Diagram

   | Birds   vs.   Other Vertebrates |
   | --- |
   | a. lighter bones |
   |    —less dense |
   |    —air sacs in bone |
   |    —smaller sex organs |
   | b. strong breast muscles |
   | c. wings and feathers |

   →   Ability to fly

   (Cause)                              (Effect)

3. Organizational pattern: time order (and contrast)
   Main idea: How Ali Kosh changed over time.
   Outline

   a. 7500 B.C. community lived mostly on wild plants and animals
   b. 5500 B.C. agriculture and herding became more important
   c. After 5500 B.C., irrigation and domesticated cattle are important

4. Organizational pattern: cause-effect (and contrast)
   Main idea: How wealth of a population affects the environment
   Diagram

   Affluent country     →     Positive effects
                              *safe drinking water
                              *sanitary sewage
                              *disposal of refuge
                              *conserve and manage parks and woodlands
                              *better agricultural practices

                              Negative effects
                              *use more fossil fuels     →     pollutes more

5. Organizational pattern: time order
   Main idea: The steps to follow for an effective presentation
   Outline

   a. Present the request or main idea
   b. Follow up with necessary detail
   c. Close with a cordial statement

6. Organizational pattern: time order
   Main idea: The process followed for understanding statistical probability
   Outline

   a. Numbers 1–1,000 are written on 1,000 slips of paper
   b. Randomly draw 15 slips without replacing them and record the numbers
   c. Replace the 15 slips
   d. Repeat a–c until 100 random samples have been obtained

### Putting It into Practice

Part 1a
Carbon cycle: Words that indicate time or order sequence: "Through . . . become," "Through . . . then move," "As this occurs." (Note: It could be argued that this is cause-and-effect.)

   a. Carbon atoms in carbon dioxide
   b. Photosynthesis
   c. Metabolism
   d. Carbon atoms in plant's body
   e. Carbon atoms consumed in food chain
   f. Carbon atoms in tissues of other organisms
   g. Repeated or carbon atoms broken down in cell respiration
   h. Carbon atoms released back into environment

**Chapter 9**   ### Activity

Answers will vary.

**Chapter 10**   ### Activity

**Survey**
1. This section talks about the role of energy in the ecosystem.
2. Topics include what matter and energy are, the different types of energy, how energy is converted from one form to another, and the energy laws.

3. Headings, bold words, italicized words, review questions, figures

**Question** (Answers will vary.)

1. How is energy involved in the functioning of the ecosystem?
2. What is matter and what is energy?
3. What are the energy laws and why are they important?

**Read** (Students should take notes on what they have read; this includes information to answer their questions as well as other important information in the section.)

**Recite** (Answers will vary.)

1. Any type of movement, growth, or activity requires energy. If there were no energy, the ecosystem would be dead.
2. Matter is anything that occupies space and has mass. Energy is the ability to move matter.
3. The first law of thermodynamics: Energy is neither created nor destroyed, but may be converted from one form to another. The second law of thermodynamics: In any energy conversion, you will end up with less usable energy than you started with. These laws are important because whenever you see something gaining potential energy, it must be coming from somewhere else. The amount of energy lost from the somewhere else is greater than the amount gained.

**Review** (Answers will vary.)

**Chapter 11**      Activity

| | |
|---|---|
| | September 22<br>Ecosystems: How They Work<br>p. 55–59 |
| Matter | What role does energy play in the ecosystem?<br>  * Universe = matter & energy<br>  * Matter = anything that occupies space and has mass<br>    • solids, liquids, gases<br>    • living & nonliving things<br>    • atoms = basic unit of matter |
| Energy | * Energy = light, heat, movement, electricity<br>    • no mass, no space<br>    • affects matter<br>      – changes position or state<br>    • = ability to move matter<br>  * Two Types of Energy<br>      1) <u>Kinetic</u> = energy in action or motion<br>        -light, heat energy, physical motion, electricity<br>      2) <u>Potential</u> = energy in storage<br>        -stretched rubber band<br>        -fuels (gasoline, etc.) = chemical energy<br>    • Changing types energy<br>        -potential → kinetic (Fig. 3-8)<br>        -kinetic → potential (charging a battery)<br>  * Measuring Energy |
| Calorie | Most common measure is the <u>calorie</u><br>    = heat needed to raise temp. of 1g. $H_2O$ 1°C<br>  <u>c</u>alories = calories<br>  <u>C</u>alories = kilocalories (= 1,000 calories) |
| Summary | No change in matter or movement of matter can occur w/out absorption or release of energy. |
| Laws of Thermodynamics | 1st Law of Thermodynamics<br>    = law of conservation of energy<br>    Energy is neither created nor destroyed, but may be converted from one form to another |

(continued)

| | |
|---|---|
| Entropy | 2nd Law of Thermodynamics<br>    In any energy conversion, you will end up with less usable energy than you started<br>    with.<br>Entropy = degree of disorder<br>    W/out energy inputs, all processes → ↑ entropy (disorder)<br>    e.g., buildings only become run-down; they don't renovate themselves.<br>*Systems will go <u>spontaneously</u> in one direction only; toward increasing entropy.<br>    Spontaneously = on their own |
| Summary | When potential E ↑, E ↓ somewhere else. (1st law)<br>Amount of E ↓ is > than E ↑. (2nd law) |